Tips and Inspirations to Empower Your Approach

Turning Problems into Opportunity

A Real-World Approach To Problem Solving

Nelson Cheng, PhD (H.C.), SRF.

To order additional copies of this book, contact
Toll Free +65 3165 7531 (Singapore)
Toll Free +60 3 3099 4412 (Malaysia)
www.partridgepublishing.com/singapore
orders.singapore@partridgepublishing.com

ISBN
978-1-5437-6891-6 (sc)
978-1-5437-6892-3 (hc)
978-1-5437-6890-9 (e)

Print information available on the last page.

03/26/2022

PARTRIDGE

Foreword

Prof. Benjamin Valdez Salas

Dr Nelson Cheng has been a close friend of mine for over two decades, and we have co-authored numerous scientific journals together with three books. He has invented numerous solutions to industrial problems.

As one of the leading inventors of Singapore, he is always looking for problems to solve. His belief in the purpose of his existence is to solve problems for the betterment of humanity is notably praiseworthy and encouraging. The book *Turning Problems into Opportunities* is another testament to validate the purpose of his existence

The book *Turning Problems into Opportunities*, in addition to being a useful tool for knowing how to solve problems, stimulates creativity and innovation. The book is designed to be tackled in any of its short but information-rich chapters without the order altering the reader's learning. It also contains a large number of examples, some of which have been arranged chronologically, and motivational quotes from the author and other thinkers. There are also stories lived by the author that allow us to perceive, through their integration into the theme, how such a life experience and the values received during family and scholar formation can influence our security for problem-solving. After reading the work, I can say that it is fascinating; it allows an agile reading and rapid assimilation of the concepts that the author tries to convey.

Having reviewed the manuscripts of *Turning Problems into Opportunities*, I find them to be practical and inspiring for working adults and students alike. The readers of *Turning Problems into Opportunities* will rise above the ordinary in their approach to problem-solving. When we read *Turning Problems into Opportunities*, we are likening conversing with one of the greatest minds in problem-solving.

It's a good value for money and worth your time to read.

Prof. Benjamin Valdez Salas
Head of Department of Corrosion and Advanced Materials
Institute of Engineering
Autonomous University of Baja California

Prof. Mario Alberto Curiel Álvarez

During this current pandemic where problems seem insurmountable, *Turning Problems into Opportunities* is a good book to read. For people of all ages, the book uses inspirational quotes and practical techniques to solve problems. In the case of busy working adults who can't read from cover to cover, the book's format allows you to pick and choose sections that are relevant to you.

By using real-life case studies, the author truly demonstrated his ability to turn problems into opportunities. A classic example of turning a problem into an opportunity is Singapore's invention of Newater, which turns sewage into drinking water in a resource-constrained environment.

A unique practical guide is highly recommended for problem-solving.

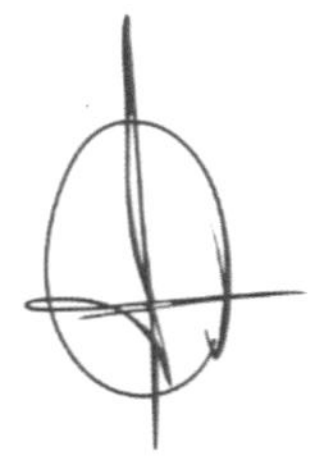

Prof. Mario Alberto Curiel Alvarez
Director of the Institute of Engineering
Autonomous University of Baja California

Prof. Ernesto A. Beltrán Partida

Dr Nelson Cheng is a Senior Honorary Research Fellow of the Autonomous University of Baja California. My co-authorship of the *Mothballing Reference Book for Onshore and Offshore Equipment* was very positive. I have co-authored three books with him and several technical papers.

I also enjoyed reading the book *Turning Problems into Opportunities*. It is a useful guide for people who are still trying to solve existential problems without progress.

If you're working on a problem-solving assignment, then this book is a great resource to share with your colleagues. It's suitable for academicians, students, researchers, and business professionals. All academicians, students, researchers, and businessmen should read this book.

Prof. Ernesto Beltran Partida
Laboratory Molecular Biology and Cancer
The Institute of Engineering
Autonomous University of Baja California

Dr Talosia Misipati Sataraka

Dr Nelson Cheng has put together amazing lessons from his personal and professional life. Woven within each page are principles applicable to every season one faces in life. Profound truth and principles drawn from Dr Cheng's life experience will lift all who feel the hopelessness that often assail life's journey. Each chapter encourages self-reflection or engages others to discuss the subject matters. Dr Cheng's journey and testimonial illustrations in this book are helpful to build confidence to face life head-on and never give in to the pressure that usually has caused many to succumb and give up. The principles covered in this fine literature are helpful in all aspects of life. It is beneficial for those in the leadership of organisations when faced with obstacles in leadership. It is also beneficial for anyone who feels life has given them a bitter pill to swallow and needed a way out. This book will lift the spirit, open the eyes, give strength to plow through, and motivate anyone to move on despite the life issues they face. The book is highly recommended and a must-read for any serious leader of organisations, church pastors, leadership in general, and anyone facing life's challenges in this tumultuous world we live in to help turn crises into opportunities. The book is full of wise advice, challenging truths, and easy-to-remember motivational quotations the author arranged to help shift one's perspective to overcome obstacles in life.

Dr Talosia Misipati Sataraka
Executive Director New Hope International Asia
National Director New Hope Japan

Preface

This book was written based on the author's life-proven experience and innovative solutions to turning problems into opportunities. It illustrates how problems can be opportunities for invention.

Throughout the book, you will learn about the genesis of the author's invention, rationale, and process, as well as how some of the problems he encountered, were turned into ground-breaking inventions that turned into profitable business opportunities.

The CEO of this company travels all around the world looking for problems to solve. Businessmen and CEOs typically try to avoid problems as much as possible. However, the author believes that to grow his business, he must know as many problems as possible and turn them into business opportunities by solving them.

Businessmen, working adults, academics, researchers, students, aspirants, and anyone interested in turning a problem into an invention or providing a solution will also find this book valuable. A person can either come up with a solution to a problem or come up with an invention based on the current circumstances of their life.

Creating a commercially viable business using your invention is also discussed. You will learn how to protect your invention through the application of a patent. Case histories of encountered problems in everyday life will be used to illustrate how problems can become inventions, resulting in new and profitable business opportunities.

A couple of case histories on how he found problems and turned them into successful businesses will be mentioned in this book.

When you follow God's will for your life, what happened today prepares you for what will happen tomorrow.

—Nelson Cheng

Acknowledgements

I am thankful for God's grace and divine guidance, without which it would be near impossible to manage a business and write this book simultaneously. Let alone within six months!

Special thanks to my lovely wife, Rosemary Lim; the completion of this book would not have been possible without her dedication and encouragement in seeing me complete it. My sincere appreciation to my daughter, Laura Cheng, for her artistic skills in designing the book covers.

My late father, Cheng Kim Bing, is to be credited with inspiring me, teaching me wisdom, and encouraging me during the early days of setting up Magna. In tribute to him and honour of him, a chapter of this book is dedicated to him.

Furthermore, I want to extend my gratitude to Mr Patrick Moe, my vice president for research, and Mr Derek Cheng, my assistant manager for research, for helping me conduct numerous laboratory tests and experiments over the years.

My sincere thanks go to Prof. Benjamin Valdez Salas, Prof. Roumen Zlatev Koytche from the Autonomous University of Baja California, and the Magna Think Tank, for the collaboration in the development of Silver Nanoparticles Hospital Grade Disinfectants and other research projects.

Lastly, I am grateful to Ms Jen of Patridge Publications, the editors, and all those involved in making this book a reality.

I will give thanks to you, Lord, with all my heart; I will tell of all your wonderful deeds.

—Psalm 9:1

Contents

Introduction

Does work-related stress bother you? This book is for you.

Every employee and business owner faces challenges at work and needs to find solutions to them. Depending on how you perceive the problems, you may feel discouraged or overwhelmed to the point that you quit your job or close your business or find a solution for the benefit of your company.

'A quitter never wins, and a winner never quits' is a valid maxim by legendary American football coach Vince Lombardi. It means that if a person keeps trying then there is always a way that he or she can choose, but once he or she stops trying then all possibilities are lost, hence, a quitter will always fail. There is no doubt that each of us has used the saying at some point in our lives, whether with our sports team, our academic work, or at work.

You have the choice now whether to be a quitter or a winner. That decision lies solely with you.

Through the narratives in this book, the author illustrates how he turned many work-related problems into business opportunities through his inventions in solving problems.

Our Minds

It's not my purpose to offer magical solutions, but I strongly believe there's one path leading to a meaningful life and a legacy. The mind is where it all begins and ends. Our thoughts and minds are powerful and cannot be underestimated.

As someone thinks within himself, so he is.

—Proverbs 23:7

In the absence of change, the mind ceases to exist.

—Nelson Cheng

A thinker builds ideas, and these ideas become the seeds of action. Action produces results. The Bible contains numerous other verses that emphasise the power of the mind. Let me encourage you to see the truth behind God's timeless words. It is your thoughts that determine your future and your legacy. Start capturing your thoughts.

I can do all this through him who gives me strength.

—Philippians 4:13

It takes only a change of thoughts to make a difference in our lives.

—Nelson Cheng

How Can This Book Benefit You?

Readers will become more self-sufficient in dealing with work-related problems after reading this book. You will not dread going to work because of work-related stress.

You will gain a greater sense of optimism at work and will not feel overwhelmed by problems.

You'll see problems as opportunities for you to demonstrate your worth to your boss, opportunities for you to help grow your company via solving existing or inherent problems.

This book shows how work-related problems are being addressed based on the proper perspective on problem-solving.

Throughout this book, the readers will learn the principle that no limit exists for human endeavour. In essence, this basic principle of belief will help readers to succeed at their workplaces, catch their bosses' attention, and ultimately get promoted.

Throughout this book, you will learn how to develop a problem-solving mindset as well as the value of persistence. Additionally, the book contains case histories of how the author solves problems.

One of the greatest gifts in life is a love of reading.

—Nelson Cheng

Despite Your Busy Schedules, Why Do You Need to Read This Book?

There is no way to overvalue the importance of reading this book both for working adults and for students. You might easily learn your way of thinking and develop your viewpoint in solving problems. It provides you with knowledge of problem-solving broadens your horizons and keeps your mind active. With it, you can solve problems more quickly, improve your perception skills, and better understand the problem you are solving, and in short, you become smarter. In addition, it enhances your focus and concentration, as well as your ability to think critically.

Those who want to venture beyond the ordinary must-read.

—Nelson Cheng

What Makes This Book So Valuable?

As you read this book, your imagination will be sparked, you will receive new ideas, your perspectives challenged, solutions provided, and wisdom shared. No matter where you are in your life, you can find a book that will add value to your personal or professional life.

It contains a lot of knowledge and will teach you valuable lessons on how to solve problems at work. In the book, you'll learn how to navigate aspects of fear of problem-solving, challenges, and virtually every aspect of life. It provides a glimpse into the cultures of ancient civilisations while revealing secrets from the past

A helpful book is a teacher, a counsellor, and your partner while solving problems.

—Nelson Cheng

How Is the Book Organised?

The book is divided into short chapters with heading in each subsections within each chapter to facilitate reading. It is not necessary to read from cover to cover; just turn to the chapter that interests you.

Uniquely written, this book is unlike any conventional book. The book is filled with inspirational quotes gleaned from the writer's years of experience solving problems. It also provides a column to jot down notes, thoughts, and ideas you may have conceived while reading a section. It is impossible to overemphasise the importance of ideas, as they are the seeds of action. Seeds must be sown for them to grow; otherwise, seeds can only remain like seeds.

There is a strong emphasis on useful, applicable information in this book, so it is designed to be both accessible and practical.

This is achieved by presenting each topic through one or more case studies, which serve as motivation for identifying relevant ideas and tools.

Several examples are provided to illustrate the most important points, and minor details are deliberately avoided.

In separate chapters, the author goes into more detail and structure to describe a particular technology, which is more useful when you want specific information once you have acquired a big picture. There are also references to further reading since these reference chapters are not exhaustive.

For every minute spent in organizing, an hour is earned.

—Benjamin Franklin

Why Should You Pick Up This Book Right Now?

My dad told me once that procrastination steals opportunities. This led me to stop procrastinating in all my endeavours, including writing this book. Time and tide wait for no one, so now is the best time since you are already in the bookstore.

Whoever watches the wind will not plant; whoever looks at the clouds will not reap.

—Ecclesiastes 11:4

Nelson Cheng, PhD (H.C.), SRF.

The power of knowledge lies in its application. You cannot find a better investment than enriching your mind by reading more. Exercise strengthens the body and reading strengthens the mind.

> *A book that you don't enjoy reading isn't the right book for you, try reading this book.*
>
> —Nelson Cheng

A Few Words from the Author

Wishing all readers of this book the best in using it, and thank you all for taking the time to read it. I hope that this book will inspire you to come up with solutions or inventions that will improve society and humankind by helping to solve problems.

Have a nice reading experience.

Best regards,

Nelson Cheng, PhD (HC), SRF

CHAPTER 1
Why Do I Look for Problems?

The Purpose of Our Existence

One of the purposes of our existence is to solve problems. We must solve society's and life's problems, to enhance humanity's well-being.

The challenge of human existence is not just staying alive but finding meaning in life.
—Nelson Cheng

A Belief of the Author

Getting to know as many problems as possible and turning them into business opportunities is the author's philosophy for growing his business. Knowing the existential problems facing each industrial sector resulted in the invention of more than 500 new products. The products invented by the author demonstrate that understanding existential problems, and solving them is the way to grow his business. Having started his business more than thirty years ago, the author has lived by this belief.

When you begin to doubt whether something is possible, it becomes impossible forever.
—Nelson Cheng

Why Do I Seek Out Problems?

You gain experiences, learn, and become wiser and stronger through challenges and problems. Challenges provide us with opportunities for growth and development. It's the hope that a life without problems is the biggest problem people have. No matter what the result is, value the experience and learn from it.

Hence, don't run from life's challenges and problems. You shouldn't try to hide them or ignore them. Deal with them by providing a solution. Taking on and overcoming a serious challenge, problem, or challenge will lead to your greatest growth and the greatest lessons you will learn.

When you doubt something about its possibility, it becomes impossible.
—Nelson Cheng

Life Is Filled with Problems

Life is full of problems as long you are breathing. Problems will inevitably crop up when studying or working, but by resolving them, you will become stronger. The fact is that problems are part of life; we must deal with them, and we either defeat them or learn to deal with them more effectively and become stronger to overcome them.

If we are still alive and kicking, we need to solve problems of all shapes and sizes. I was instilled with the belief that this is the truth by my late beloved father, Cheng Kim Bing. This truth I still embrace to date.

Sunrise or hope could never be overcome by a problem.

—Nelson Cheng

All problems can be overcome by hope of solving it.

—Nelson Cheng

Our Entire Existence Is a Process of Solving Existential Problems

Throughout history, mankind has been looking for solutions to many problems under the great blue sky, since the dawn of the age of man. Have we ever thought to look at the one place where we can find them: the human mind?

During your first eight months of life, you faced several challenges, of which survival was one of the most important. While you might not remember, there was a point when you could no longer remain in the safety of your mother's womb. After propelling through a birth canal, it was necessary to fill your lungs with enough air to keep your bloodstream supplied with oxygen. You made your very first cry and took your very first breath instinctively; the mysterious problem of breathing was solved. Here you are, several years later, trying to decipher why you need to learn how to deal with problems.

Well, if it can be thought, it can be done, a problem can be overcome.

—E. A. Bucchianeri

Having Problems Is Inevitable in Life

Either you seek the problem out and provide a solution by nabbing at its bud or you wait passively to be sought out by it. Every single one of us is either having a problem right now, has just emerged from one, or is about to have one.

Problems are best avoided by solving them; hence, it is better to solve your problems than to run away from them.

The absence of cause does not exist. Nothing happens by accident. The causes of problems and their effects will accompany us no matter where we are, who we are, how old we are; therefore, do run away from problems. Seek them, face it, and solve it. That is why I look for problems and provide many solutions to become one of Singapore's leading inventors.

All I have seen teaches me to trust the Creator for all I have not seen.

—Ralph Waldo Emerson

Is there anything I learned from looking for problems in chapter 1?

What should I do to resolve my problem?

CHAPTER 2

The Importance for Defining a Problem

Definition of a Problem

A problem is something difficult to deal with: something that is a source of trouble, worry, etc. An intricate unsettled question. A source of perplexity, distress, or vexation. From the Greek word *problēma*, which means 'obstacle'.

Albert Einstein's Wise Words

Albert Einstein once said, *'If I were given one hour to save the planet, I would spend fifty-nine minutes defining the problem and one minute resolving it.'*

The words Einstein uttered were wise, but from my experience, most people or organisations ignore them when considering solutions to their problems. Most people or organisations fail to fully define the problems they're trying to solve and explain why those issues are important when developing solutions, new products, processes, or even businesses.

By not defining the problem, people and organisations miss opportunities, waste resources, and pursue initiatives that aren't aligned with their strategic goals. Many times, you will discover in hindsight that a new path should have been taken after a project takes one path.

A seemingly innovative program may deliver a seemingly breakthrough result, but it may not be able to be implemented, or it may address an incorrect problem. To solve the right problems, people or organisations need to become better at asking the right questions so that they can tackle the right problems.

In the Face of a Problem, Why Should a Problem Statement Be Written?

If a problem is defined well, it is already half-solved. To fix a sum, you must go back until you pinpoint the error, then work from there, never by simply continuing.

Hence, an articulation of the problem or issues the project strives to address is a problem statement. As part of the problem statement, you identify the current state, the desired future state, and any gaps between the two. It is important for everyone involved in a project to understand what the problem they need to solve is and why this project is of importance by defining the problem in a problem statement.

In a process improvement project, the problem statement plays a significant role in identifying the project's goals and outlining its scope. The activities and decisions of the project participants can also be guided by it. Business or organisation leaders can use the problem statement to gain buy-in and support for process improvement initiatives.

Science is true whether or not one believes in it.

—Nelson Cheng

How Should a Problem Statement Be Constructed?

When formulating a problem statement, there are four crucial components you should include: the ideal situation, the actuality, the consequence, and the plan.

The Ideal Scenario

You should start by describing what the ideal scenario would be if you didn't have any problems to solve. Here you should describe what the project aims and how it will be managed. After the issue has been resolved, this section should provide a clear picture of what the ideal environment will be.

The Actuality

You should describe what the current situation is at your company or organisation in the next part of your problem statement. In this section, the problem will be identified, explained as to why it is a problem, and who is impacted by the problem. In addition, the section will explain when and where the problem was identified.

The Consequence

You should then describe the consequences of the problem in the next part of your problem statement. The purpose of this section is to describe how the effects of the problem are affecting the people affected by it. It also measures how much of an impact it has on them. Among the multitude of consequences are the loss of time, money, resources, competitive advantage, productivity, and more.

The Plan

There may be several possible solutions in the plan section of a problem statement, but it is imperative to note that it doesn't have to identify a specific solution. Project team members should use the proposal section to guide their research, investigation, and solution.

> *Give me six hours to chop down a tree and I will spend the first four sharpening the axe.*
> —Abraham Lincoln

How Should a Problem Statement Be Written?

The most effective solution to any problem statement is to identify and answer several related questions. An ideal approach to drafting a problem statement is to use the questioning method.

The questioning method entails identifying *what* the problem is, *why* it is a problem, *when* and *where* it was detected, *who* it impacts, *how* it impacts them, and *how* significant the impact is of the problem. The following steps can be used to craft a problem statement that addresses the following:

1. Determine the cause of the problem.
2. Write the ideal scenario at the beginning of your statement.
3. Explain where the current gaps are.
4. What are the possible consequences of the problem?
5. Plans for arresting the problem

Determine the Cause of the Problem

To write your problem statement, first, you need to determine what the problem is.

Write Your Ideal Scenario at the Start of Your Statement

Next, you can begin writing your problem statement by describing what the ideal environment would look like if the problem didn't exist. This section should try to describe what your company hopes to accomplish because of the process improvement project.

Explain the Current Gaps

The next step is to write the actual problem statement. The current environment must be described clearly in this section. It is the purpose of this section to identify the problem, what is causing it, and why it is a problem. Determining the problem also requires describing when, where, and how you identified it.

What Are the Possible Consequences of the Problem?

After that, you should write a section on the consequences of your problem statement. The purpose of this section is to quantify the problem and provide evidence to support that claim. This section allows you to identify specific numbers, such as the amount of time or revenue wasted, or the resources wasted. You must include concrete numbers in this section that demonstrate your claim.

Plans for Arresting the Problem

A section on the proposal should be included at the end of your statement. Describe how your company plans to achieve your goals and achieve a desirable environment in this section. While your company may identify several potential solutions in this section, the focus needs to be on determining how those solutions will be discovered than on identifying the solution.

Charles Franking Kettering, a famous American engineer, businessman, and inventor, once said, *'A problem well stated is a problem half solved.'*

Since some of the biggest breakthroughs in history have happened due to well-defined problems, this statement does not need any validation.

Define your problem by writing down your problem statement on the following lines.

Determine the cause of the problem.

Write down any conceived thoughts for action.

CHAPTER 3

Author's Experience in Problem-Solving

Solving Manufacturing Problems

I started out focusing on highly specific technical problems in manufacturing but have since expanded to cover everything from basic research and product development to the health and safety of each industry.

To find a suitable solution for each industry, the thoroughness with which a problem is faced by each industry is defined and is crucial. Unfortunately, most organisations struggle to articulate their problems clearly and concisely. Most organisations or people struggle to identify which problems are most important to their missions or strategies.

Our children will not learn if we instantly provide them with answers instead of problems to solve.

—Nelson Cheng

Barking Up the Wrong Tree

Our clients frequently learn while working with us that they are not addressing the right problem due to a lack of clarity in defining the problem. Lack of clear definition is akin to an attempt or pursuit of a futile course of action in problem-solving by barking up the wrong tree.

Harmony rests on the clarity of one's mind.

—Nelson Cheng

Problem Definition

Analyse the situation so that you focus your attention on the problem and not just its symptoms. Flowcharts help identify the expected steps of a process, and cause-and-effect diagrams are useful to identify and analyse the root causes of problems.

You can accomplish anything if you have motivation, and focus.

—Nelson Cheng

Problem-Definition Process

A lot of questions need to be asked during the problem-definition process. What are the causes of the problem? When did it arise? How can it be resolved? Who is responsible for the solution? What is the best approach? What resources are required to solve the problem? How will it be resolved? In what timeframe will the problem be solved?

By following these steps, interested parties are involved, factual information is used, expectations are compared to reality, and the root causes of a problem are explored. To begin, you should review the documentation of current processes (i.e., who does what, with what information, with what tools, communicating with whom, in what timeframe, using what format). Analyse how new tools and revised policies may impact the development of your model of 'what should be'.

An assessment of a man should be based on his questions, not his answers.

—Nelson Cheng

What Are the Causes of the Problem?

It is important to understand the cause of a problem before identifying and selecting appropriate options to solve it. Obtaining such insights may also enable an alternative framing of the problem to be selected. It is unlikely that determining the cause or underlying factors will be a simple process. In addition to reducing uncertainty about the cause, it may be equally or even more important to clarify that uncertainty.

The ability to deal with problems is the key to happiness, not the absence of problems.

—Nelson Cheng

What Are the Root Causes of the Problem?

Problems or issues have root causes. These are the fundamental reasons behind them. The problem-solving process should include trying to determine why an issue has developed to ensure the right response is given to help solve the problem.

It's always challenging in solving a problem. Although the 'But why?' method may not always be the best approach and should not be used 100 per cent of the time. The technique is a quick and inexpensive way to locate a variety of solutions and can be used by anyone, anywhere, at any time. However, in some cases, you should use more sophisticated methods, such as surveys, interviews, and data collection.

It is important to note that a proposed solution to address the problem will fail when people are ignorant or deny the cause of the problem.

To progress, one must overcome problems, not simply avoid them.

—Nelson Cheng

Problem Sources vs. Problem Causes

The cause is not the source of the problem. To identify the causes, we must think deeper. A symptom is just the source of a problem. For example, we are hampered by today's urgent needs, whether they reduce productivity or interrupt our way of life. We should attend to the urgent issues, but the truly important issue is what needs the most attention.

In the process of identifying the source and causes of a problem, one of the commonest mistakes made is the way to see a problem that is the main problem. Most people pay attention to urgent issues, but they should not eclipse their complete focus that will lose sight of the cause source and the source.

Difficulties cannot be avoided; they must be overcome.

—Nelson Cheng

What did I learn from Author's experience in chapter 2?

What are some ways I can apply it in my situations?

CHAPTER 4
The Essentials of Problem-Solving

One must overcome problems, not simply avoid them.

—Nelson Cheng

Hope

Let's look at what are the essentials of developing a solution in this chapter. Developing an effective solution begins with the mind. The mind is our battleground whether we are successful in figuring out a solution or defeated by a problem.

A mind filled with hope is powerful. Hope will allow you to realise your dreams, visions, and endeavours.

We must fortify our minds with hope before a solution can be developed. In so many different areas of our life, hope helps us to develop our mental muscles, which, in turn, will help us immensely in problem-solving.

Through it, hope will be able to help us overcome challenges, bounce back quickly from failures, and see challenges as opportunities to grow.

Hope always allows a person to find a way to solve a problem, but when a person loses hope, all possibilities disappear. Ultimately, failure is inevitable.

The mind can adapt and change when it is constantly filled with hope. It is important to continue stretching your brain muscles and retaining your mental strength with hope. You can remain mentally strong throughout your life if you fortify your mind with hope.

The power of hope cannot be understated. When we face difficult times, it inspires us to do the impossible.

—Nelson Cheng

Persistency

The second essential for developing a solution for problem-solving is persistence. To persist is probably one of the most admirable traits a person can have. Having the determination to persevere regardless of setbacks is what makes it possible to do or achieve something.

Mastering persistence is one of the keys to success in solving problems, individuals who succeed in life have persistent qualities that distinguish them from those who don't.

Even though many can set goals and make plans towards success, only a few succeed because only a few people persist in their work until the goal is achieved.

Most people stop before they start or quit midway through their journey. It is not uncommon for people to quit due to hardships, discomfort, and uncertainty. Instead of persisting towards their goals, they let their fears and doubts paralyse them. Possibly, their motivation is not strong enough to spur them to move forward.

The time has come for you to learn how to master persistence if you desire change in your life.

The power of persistence is omnipotent.

—Nelson Cheng

And let us not grow weary of doing good, for in due season we will reap if we do not give up.

—Galatians 6:9

Self-Discipline

The goal of self-discipline is to create new habits in thought, behaviour, and speech so that you improve yourself and reach your goals in problem-solving.

Self-discipline is what bridges problems and solutions; problem-solving and solutions are connected by self-discipline. Developing self-discipline is crucial to achieving solutions to your problems.

To be disciplined, you need to leave your comfort zone. A habit is something you want to change, not something you want to sweat through. It requires discipline and thought to forego immediate pleasure. Specifically, self-discipline involves keeping yourself focused on what needs to be done to achieve your goal by solving the problem.

When self-discipline is present, most things are possible.

—Nelson Cheng

No discipline seems pleasant at the time, but painful. Later, however, it produces a harvest of righteousness and peace for those who have been trained by It.

—Hebrews 12:11

Comfort Zone Inhibits Creativity

A comfort zone is an environment in which people feel at ease and are in control of their environment, exhibiting low levels of anxiety and stress. When people are in this zone, they can maintain just a steady performance level, not exceptional performance.

When a person is in a comfort zone, things feel familiar to them, and they feel at ease and perceive they are in control of their surroundings or problems, hence, experiencing low levels of anxiety and stress. In this state, they can never experience peak performance as the saying goes familiarity breeds contempt. It remains true that when one gets too attached to or familiar with something, there is no extraordinary solution possible if one loses respect for it.

Leaving your comfort zone is one of the essentials in problem-solving. We must not be intimidated by the fear of the unknown and stick to old ways in solving problems. Albert Einstein once said, 'The definition of insanity is doing the same thing over and over again and expecting different results.'

For God gave us a spirit not of fear but of power and love and self-control.
—2 Timothy 1:7

Stepping outside of your comfort zone is the first step toward change.
—Nelson Cheng

Develop a Strong Mindset

In every situation of problem-solving, your attitude is determined by your mindset. Our minds are powerful, and they create forces. It is only by having a strong mindset that you will succeed. Having a strong mindset helps you feel more confident and see challenges as opportunities, successes as steppingstones to more success, and failures as a chance to learn and grow.

Having a strong positive mindset restores your belief in your abilities, capacities, and talents. They can have a big impact on your self-esteem in problem-solving. With time, you'll be able to accomplish your dream career.

The legendary boxer Muhammad Ali once said, 'I told myself I was the greatest, even before I knew I was.'

You will see a change in the outside world once your mindset changes.
—Nelson Cheng

Once you change your mind, you'll begin to see a difference in the outside world.
—Nelson Cheng

Moving Forward

In life, intentions are not what matters, but action.

—Nelson Cheng

Keep moving forward every day, no matter what pace you choose to solve your problems. Make it a daily goal to do something to solve these problems, no matter how busy you are.

By moving forward, you will be in motion, not static. You will be progressing, which will, in turn, motivate you to spend more time solving the problem. Moving closer to providing a solution to your problem.

'How do you eat an elephant? One bite at a time,' a popular saying has it.

A man can swallow an elephant one bite at a time if he puts his mind to it and doing so will make him a bigger and stronger man. In any event, he cannot swallow it all at once and must reject the ivory.

The reason so many people fail to realise their dreams or solve their problems is because of this experience. They try to eat an elephant in one bite. Taking smaller steps at a time will allow a giant task or a problem to be accomplished or solved.

It's important to set a goal for yourself to eat the elephant as it should be eaten. I'm a big fan of goals, as anyone who knows me or has worked with me will testify. The evidence I've seen in my life and work has convinced me that human beings are capable of far more than we can imagine.

The first step in realising our limitless potential is to know what it is we wish to accomplish when solving a problem. A life that is meaningful, fulfilling, and success begins with setting goals. In general, goal setting plays a significant role in problem-solving.

In life, actions matter more than intentions.

—Nelson Cheng

But you shall remember the Lord your God, for it is He who is giving you the power to make wealth, that He may confirm His covenant which He swore to your fathers, as it is this day.

—Deuteronomy 8:18

What are the attributes mentioned in chapter 3 that I need to develop?

What must I do to develop those missing attributes in problem-solving?

CHAPTER 5
The Process of Problem-Solving

Steps to the Process of Problem-Solving

Once you have mastered the essentials of problem-solving, you begin the process. The process of problem-solving includes taking steps to accomplish a particular result or producing something.

Learning is a process, and one level leads to another.

—Nelson Cheng

There are many ways in which solving problems differs based on how one approaches new concepts and responds effectively to opportunities solving them.

—Nelson Cheng

Step 1: Consider All Possible Solutions

Consider all possible solutions once you understand the issue at hand. Most problems can be solved in several ways. Don't overlook any possibilities. Feedback and collaboration are also vital here.

The impossible is possible as long as you don't know it is impossible.

—Nelson Cheng

Step 2: Identify the Most Appropriate Solution

Identify the most appropriate solution for those involved. The cost and benefits of a given solution will need to be addressed in a business. To solve problems in an educational setting, you may want to ask professors or mentors what they think will be most effective.

No matter what the problem, you can be part of the solution.

—Nelson Cheng

Step 3: Put into Practice the Chosen Solution

Once you've chosen a solution to a problem, it's imperative that you put it into practice. Otherwise, you will have to solve the problem again. Be persistent! Resilience comes from overcoming challenges.

It is common for people to be enthusiastic, but it is rare for them to be resilient.

—Nelson Cheng

Step 4: Listen Actively to What Others Say

Meanwhile, you should actively listen to your team members. There is a substantial difference between hearing and actively listening. To participate in active listening, the listener must pay undivided attention to the speaker. When you use active listening, you maximise problem-solving skills, since you can understand what someone is trying to say.

We learn by listening, not by talking.

—Nelson Cheng

Step 5: Exercise Your Analytical Skills

A problem-solving process requires analytical skills. A problem can be understood and viewed in different ways by everyone. It's possible to come up with the best solutions when you think critically about what's going on.

The analysis of a problem leads to the creation of a solution.

—Nelson Cheng

Step 6: Using Available Research Data

Big data is becoming increasingly important to the process of problem-solving. By using data and research, it is possible to predict the solutions to the problems before they even take place.

I would rather have a little data than none at all.

—Nelson Cheng

Step 7: Creative Thinking

The problem-solving process involves creative thinking. The process of creative thinking is about developing your imagination and thinking outside the box. Innovating, solving problems, creating, and communicating in fresh, new ways are all possible with the ability to think creatively.

There are times when you will have constraints to solve a problem. These constraints could be what's causing the problem in the first place. Creativity is key in overcoming such challenges.

Imagination is the seed of creation.

—Nelson Cheng

Step 8: Communication during the Process of Problem-Solving

You will be able to get your team's contribution if you talk about problems and accurately describe their origins during the process of problem-solving. Effective communication can speed up problem-solving in this way.

Wisdom comes from having something to say, and foolishness arises from having to say something, hence, the difference between wisdom and foolishness is having something to say and having to say something.

—Nelson Cheng

Step 9: Implementing the Solution

Since challenges can have multiple solutions, you will need to determine which solution will be implemented. The solution that is practical, economical, and agreed by the team should be implemented

It's easy to think of ideas, but it is hard to implement them.

—Nelson Cheng

The first step to solving my problem is to determine the immediate steps I need to take.

Using the problem-solving process, what is the first problem I want to address?

CHAPTER 6

The Process of Problem-Solving for an Organisation

Whether a person's decisions are based on facts or follow public opinion determines whether they are wise or ignorant.

—Nelson Cheng

To run and manage a successful organisation, leadership must guide their employees and develop problem-solving skills. The following problem-solving process and methodology outlined below can find a suitable solution for any issue your organisation is facing.

Distinguish Between Fact and Opinion during Problem-Solving

It is imperative to differentiate fact from opinion when solving problems within an organisation. Whether based on facts or public opinion, wise and ignorant leaders take different approaches to making decisions.

Opinions are formed about something without necessarily being based on facts or knowledge. Based on nothing more than feelings, an opinion is an interpretation of something, not necessarily based on knowledge.

A fact is based on a proven or known truth, a piece of information presented as having objective reality something that has actual existence.

Verifiability, the ability to demonstrate that a statement of fact corresponds to experience, is usually the test of a statement of fact. Usually, facts are checked against standard reference books. A fact is verified by repeatable careful observation or measurement through experiments or other methods.

The ability to distinguish fact from opinion is essential for leaders and workers. Unfortunately, it is often difficult to tell the two apart. To effectively implement these principles, leaders and workers in an organisation must understand their definitions well. Once leaders and workers understand the definitions, they can apply them to a wide range of topics

Why Is It Important to Consider Facts and Opinions?

To avoid being easily deceived, it is essential to distinguish between what is fact and what is an opinion, regardless of the source of information that is used during problem-solving.

Being able to differentiate between fact and opinion can also help leaders and workers in an organisation develop logical and analytical skills. There is often a mix of fact and opinion in writings and statements.

> *Our ability to distinguish what is real (fact) from what is simply belief (opinion) is imperative if we are to successfully handle the tsunami of opinions out there.*
>
> —Nelson Cheng

Having learned the importance of facts and opinions, you must now be able to distinguish them. Many facts are accompanied by an opinion. A challenge sometimes arises when separating verifiable data from one's own biases and personal preferences.

How to Differentiate Fact from an Opinion?

The terminology people use often provides useful clues, such as terms and phrases that help us differentiate between factual and opinion-based claims. Often, fact or opinion statements are accompanied by signal words and phrases that can be found in sentence fragments. Below are a few examples of fact statements and opinion statements.

Fact Statements

'Recent research has identified . . .'

'Based on the findings of the investigation . . .'

'The review of the literature indicates . . .'

'The most recent report confirms . . .'

Opinion Statements

'From my point of view . . .'

'It is believed that . . .'

'According to the officer . . .'

'It was concluded that . . .'

From the above examples, it is possible to determine whether a statement is being presented as a fact or an opinion based on the terminology used.

Likewise, it is important for individuals to understand that things are not always what they seem. We often frame opinions as facts and vice versa, whether consciously or unconsciously. It is therefore imperative that we develop a solid understanding of the difference between fact and opinion as well as sufficient practice distinguishing them.

How Can Fact and Opinion Be Further Distinguished?

In addition to understanding the differences between a fact and an opinion, it is also important that we can distinguish the two when reading literature. We'll examine a few useful strategies now.

Watch Out for Opinions Disguised as Facts

To the untrained eye, technical or professional terminology can also appear factual. Especially interesting are predictions. Predictions cannot yet be verified, so they are considered opinions. There is no difference between who makes the prediction.

A marine biologist who predicts the extinction of a plant species in fifty years, for instance, is expressing an educated opinion. This opinion is based on proof, analysis, and experience, but it is not a fact because it cannot be verified at this time.

Expressions of Judgement or Value Often Imply a Point of View

Singaporeans are really very wealthy. Most people will agree with this comment. However, the term *really* complicates things.

What does it mean to be very wealthy? It hasn't been identified. What one person considers wealthy may be considered average by another.

Furthermore, the word *very* is a judgement word. Below are a few value and judgement terms to look for in a statement; if one of these terms appears, it is likely a viewpoint:

'The worst . . .'

'The greatest . . .'

'The most . . .'

'The prettiest . . .'

'The loveliest . . .'

Be Aware of Words Like *Should* or *Ought To*

Occasionally, these terms refer to suggestions or recommendations. These suggestions are always helpful, but they are rarely accurate. Any 'should' argument, no matter how strongly we agree with it, is still just an opinion.

For example, 'One should stop smoking cigarettes' may be a sensible piece of advice backed by plenty of evidence, but it is still merely a personal opinion. By contrast, the statement, 'Smoking cigarettes causes several health problems', is verifiable.

Opportunities present themselves when big challenges arise.

—Nelson Cheng

Is there anything I have learned from problem-solving in an organisation?

CHAPTER 7

How to Handle a Problem That Has No Solution?

If a problem has no solution, it may not be a problem, but a fact—
not to be solved, but to be coped with over time.

—Shimon Peres, Ninth President of the State of Israel

Without a Solution, How Should a Problem Be Classified?

According to Israel's ninth president, Shimon Peres, a problem that cannot be solved is not for you to solve, but for you to cope with.

We most likely speak of reality here. Occasionally, life will present us with unexpected situations. These situations will not require us to look for solutions since they can only be resolved by accepting life as it is. We must accept these situations as they present themselves.

With No Solution, How Can We Handle the Problem?

We are inhibiting our ability to find the best solution to a problem when we obsess over it to the point of worrying about it excessively. It is as if we have a veil covering our eyes, preventing us from seeing further and inhibiting us from thinking.

Thus, to find the most effective solution, we must put distance between ourselves and the problem, take a step back from what we are used to, and analyse the problem from a different perspective.

Our creativity must be enhanced, as well as our openness to new perspectives on the situation. This opens new horizons and new possibilities, creating new solutions in coping with it.

Our minds need to expand when we confront a problem without a solution, and we need to remain calm and emotionally balanced when facing a problem without a solution.

We benefit from seeing our problems from a different perspective and breaking away for a little while, allowing us to give ourselves real space. Additionally, it frees us from stressful situations that can prevent us from finding solutions.

An example of a problem without a solution:

Land Scarcity of Singapore

There appears to be no solution to Singapore's land scarcity problem, so its people have adapted to cope with it.

When one talks of a problem without a solution, Singapore faces a unique challenge. There are 718.3 km^2 of land in the city-state, and its population is continually growing.

Despite this, it has been more successful in improving housing standards in the past fifty years than in any other country. Despite having scarce land, roads in Singapore are much less congested than in comparable cities. This has not always been the case. Singapore's city core was overcrowded in 1960, even though it housed only 1.63 million people. Today, the city-state has more than 5.9 million residents.

What Did Singapore Do to Overcome Its Land Shortage?

Listed below are five ways Singapore overcame its land shortage and what other countries can learn from them:

The Reclamation of Land

Reclamation, of course, cannot be a long-term strategy to get around shortages because it has a finite amount of land. Singapore, however, increased its land supply by reclaiming land from the sea. In Singapore, for example, the sea has been filled with imported sand since independence, increasing land supply by 20 per cent. This will result in an 8 per cent increase in supply. Singapore's largest outlying island, Jurong Island, was formed by the amalgamation of seven offshore islands.

Putting Up Buildings Underground

Human beings are innovative, and when there is no space above ground, they will dig underground. In Singapore, there are underground ammunition facilities and underground oil storage facilities. For example, Singapore's underground ammunition storage facilities are the first of their kind in the world, and the country's underground oil storage facilities are the first in Southeast Asia.

Integrated Projects

In Singapore, integrated projects have reduced land consumption by lowering commute times, and by efficiently utilising land. Real estate developers can also benefit from the existing infrastructure with mixed-use projects in the city centre. Supply and demand will be better synchronised as a result. Those living in mixed-use neighbourhoods are also more likely to be near their workplaces and amenities. Consequently, fewer road spaces and other property assets are consumed.

Planning an Integrated Urban Environment

The success of Singapore's urban planning is by no means a coincidence. Infrastructure projects that were not strategically placed or districts not connected to other districts with complementary functions would have resulted in inefficient land use.

After independence, Singapore's leaders began planning the city's infrastructure. The housing blocks became complexes, and the primary functions of cities were centralised. There is less reliance on roads because the Mass Rapid Transit System links all districts, reducing the need for road space. Land-use planning and transport are integrated in Singapore, which is one of the few countries that does this. The city state has also succeeded in enforcing congestion pricing. Industries are located where they do not pollute rivers and lakes.

Construction of a High-Density Building

Singapore's central business district has a floor area ratio (the ratio of floor space to plot area) of twenty-five. In most Indian cities, the floor space to plot area ranges from one to two. The integration of land use and transport planning was enabled by high-density buildings.

The city has also become more vibrant since this has allowed more people to migrate there. Highly skilled migrants are largely responsible for Singapore's development. A high density of buildings enabled the land-scarce city-state to have more green space and open spaces.

It is imperative that our creativity and openness to new perspectives on the situation are enhanced. It opens new horizons and new possibilities, leading to new ways of coping with a problem without a solution.

> *To the young and to the not so old, I say, look at that horizon, follow that rainbow, go ride it.*
> —Lee Kuan Yew, the longest-serving prime minister in the world

> *Life is not just eating, drinking, television and cinema . . . The human mind must be creative, must be self-generating; it cannot depend on just gadgets to amuse itself.*
> —Lee Kuan Yew, 1959–1970, speech at Chinese New Year and Hari Raya Haji Celebrations held at Joo Seng Community Centre, 28 February 1970

What must I do when a problem has no solution?

CHAPTER 8
Inspiration and Problem-Solving

What Is Inspiration?

It can be defined as something that makes someone want to do something or that gives someone an idea about what to do or create, a force or influence that inspires someone.

The Myth of Inspiration

Inspiration is often overlooked due to its elusive nature. The fact that it is thought to be supernatural or divine hasn't helped. Recent research, however, shows that inspiration can be activated, captured, and manipulated, and it has a profound effect on our lives.

Success and inspiration are connected.

—Nelson Cheng

The Importance of Inspiration

We will examine why inspiration is so critical to solving problems in this chapter.

As society is obsessed with measuring talent and ability, we often overlook the role inspiration plays. Our everyday experiences and limitations are transcended by inspiration when it awakens us to new possibilities. We perceive ourselves differently after being inspired and moving from apathy to possibility.

Our ordinary experiences and limitations are transcended by inspiration, and we are propelled from apathy to possibility. Inspiration plays a crucial role in solving problems, yet it is often overlooked.

In the first place, inspiration occurs spontaneously, without intention. The second, inspiration transcends our animalistic and egoistic concerns and limitations and often involves a sense of clarity and realisation of new possibilities.

In the human spirit, we are motivated by inspiration that precedes us, which opens our eyes to greater possibilities. It often manifests as a clear vision or a glimpse of something one has never seen before but has probably always been there.

In addition, inspiration involves self-motivation, in which the individual tries to transfer, express, or actualise a new idea or vision. In other words, both inspiration and action involve being inspired by something and acting upon that inspiration.

Inspiration allows us to see possibilities beyond our ordinary experiences and limitations.

—Nelson Cheng

Benefits of Inspiration

Based on my observation, people who were inspired had higher levels of absorption in their assigned task during problem-solving and were more open to new ideas and experiences. Generally, openness to experience comes before inspiration, suggesting that those who are more open to experiencing inspiration are more likely to experience it. Additionally, inspired individuals weren't more conscientious, supporting the notion that inspiration is something that happens to you.

Inspiration and creativity are intertwined.

—Nelson Cheng

Progress towards Goals Is Made Easier by Inspiration

According to research carried out from Carleton University, college students were asked to state three goals they planned to achieve during the semester. Reports were then submitted three times per month. As a result of setting more inspired goals, those who scored higher on the inspiration scale showed better goal progress. Therefore, inspiration in daily life resulted in setting more inspiring goals, which were then more likely to be achieved by those who were more inspired.

In addition, goal progress predicted future inspiration for future goals: it was reciprocal between inspiration and goal progress. This implies that progress towards goals and inspiration are correlated, resulting in a cycle of greater goal inspiration and pursuit of goals. Finally, inspired individuals reported living their lives with greater purpose and gratitude.

Any successful person must be inspired.

—Nelson Cheng

The Intrinsic Value of Inspiration

Inspired individuals tended to exhibit more intrinsic motivation and less extrinsic motivation, variables that also significantly influence their work performance. The influence of inspirational variables on creativity was least dependent on factors involving agency or the enhancement of resources, again indicating that inspiration is transcendent.

Inspired individuals have also been found to possess a greater level of important psychological resources such as self-confidence, self-esteem, and optimism, which are indispensable in problem-solving.

There is more inspiration among patent holders than among non-patent holders, and the number of patents held increases with the frequency of inspiration. The creativity of inspired people appears to increase over time, as measured by increased self-ratings as time goes by.

Inspiration and success are correlated.

—Nelson Cheng

But the Helper, the Holy Spirit, whom the Father will send in my name, he will teach you all things and bring to your remembrance all that I have said to you.

—John 14:26

What benefits do I get if I solved my current problems?

What are the benefits I can take advantage of?

CHAPTER 9
Transforming Problems into Opportunities for Inventions

Transforming problems into opportunity begins with changing our perceptions.

—Nelson Cheng

Opportunities present themselves when big challenges arise.

—Nelson Cheng

The Right Perspective for Problem-Solving

If we have the right perspective for problem-solving, we can turn problems into opportunities for invention.

It is important that you always see workplace problems as opportunities for the company's growth, as opportunities for you to provide solutions, as opportunities to show the company your worth as an employee, or as opportunities to showcase your significance to the company. The right perspective is what motivates you to seek a solution. To find new ideas that will eventually lead to inventions, the right perspective is crucial to problem-solving.

By changing our perception of problems, we can turn them into opportunities.

—Nelson Cheng

In the face of problems, perspective matters a great deal.

—Nelson Cheng

What Is an Invention?

In short, invention is the creation of something new.

The term *invention* refers to a new or unique device, method, composition, or process. Inventing is one component of the product development process. This could be the improvement of a machine or product or the creation of a new process. Radical breakthroughs are those inventions that solve a problem or produce a completely new result.

Another definition is an invention that builds on what came before; it is the result of continuous evolution. While it is possible to experience a stroke of genius, these moments rarely occur in isolation.

Inventions that take previous ideas and find new ways to add value that customers love are often the best ones. Remember that you do not have to start from scratch every time an innovation is thought of in your company.

The drive to create something new and revolutionary is what makes invention possible.

—Nelson Cheng

Definition of an Inventor

To invent is to come up with something new. The term comes from one of the Latin words *invenire*, meaning 'to discover, to come upon', thus an inventor is someone who comes up with something new. Science and engineering contribute significantly to inventing, but not all inventors are scientists or engineers. Many inventors are not scientists or engineers and are not necessarily trained in these fields.

It is the inventor's nature to do unexpected things.

—Nelson Cheng

It Is Not Always the Same Inventor Who Creates All Inventions

Usually, an invention is the work of several people who have collaborated. One such example is the invention of the writer's silver nanoparticles range of hospital-grade disinfectants. Two members of Magna Think Tank, Prof. Benjamin Valdez Salas and Prof. Roumen Zlatev Koytche, developed the silver nanoparticles generator, and the writer synthesised the said nanoparticles and combined it with chlorhexidine gluconate and quaternary ammonium compound to produce a range of hospital-grade disinfectants, the range of the products in other chapters of the book.

We wouldn't be able to advance much if we constructed reality around what we already believe to be true.

—Nelson Cheng

Is there a problem I am facing right now?

What opportunities are available to me if I resolve them?

CHAPTER 10

What Leads Me and Others to Invent Things?

The Purpose of Existence

Every person on this planet has a purpose, and God placed them here for a reason. I always feel that we do not exist on this planet for no reason. The quest to solve problems has been my life motto ever since this thought came into my mind. I start all my inventions thinking the *why*, *what*, and *how* questions.

I believe in solving problems after seeking them, otherwise, I am not fulfilling the purpose of my existence.

—Nelson Cheng

My quest for asking 'why' will never wane regardless of my age, and that 'retirement' is not in my vocabulary.

Learning stops when we stop asking 'Why?'

—Nelson Cheng

Why Do People Invent Things in Solving Problems?

There is a reason why a person does this, and it is an individual thing. Two of the most common reasons are to make money or because they love their idea.

Based on the number of invention patents applied for each year and the number of unpatented inventions, it appears that inventive activity around the world is high. The process of invention and the creation of revolutionary products can be framed in several ways. I will analyse first what motivates individuals to innovate and then what motivates organisations to innovate.

Almost all innovations are developed and commercialised due to economic incentives, but inventions are often the result of inventors' interests and motivations, creative thought processes, and personal make-up.

Inventors usually do so because they are curious about science and technology. They see the need to improve the features of existing products and inventors who want to help others.

For me, it's because I saw a need that I can meet and want to make a difference in the world with my invention. Being able to solve problems has become my life's credo. The more I learn, the more I read, the more I understand and acquire knowledge, and the more I can help others.

What Is the Purpose of the Invention While Solving a Problem?

For technological and human progress, inventions serve a critical purpose while solving a problem. An easy and happy life would be preferable to a tough and miserable one. Any invention that can lead to partial ease and relief of misery is important and for this reason, the invention is imperative to the progress of humanity.

If necessity is the mother of invention, urgency is the uncle of change.
Without it, progress slows and then stops and then reverses.

—Neil Scovell

What Is the Importance of Solving Problems through Inventions in Society?

If we do not continuously solve problems, improve our products, and develop new technologies, we die sooner, work harder, are more depressed, have fewer options, and are more vulnerable to poverty, starvation, and deprivation.

It is extremely important for the society we live in to continuously solve problems through inventions.

Successful inventors invent what people need; consumers
buy what the successful inventors invented.

—Nelson Cheng

Inventions Improve the Standard of Living of Society

Human progress and technological advancement are powered by inventions. Modern technologies have simplified our lives in many ways. Consider a world without a refrigerator or washing machine. Keeping some foods at home and doing the washing by hand would be impossible. Once these things were invented and distributed, it became easier to live. It can be argued that a happy, easy life is preferred over a miserable, difficult one. By this definition, an invention improves the standard of living of society by reducing misery and making life a little easier. It's for this reason we need inventions.

As education is the key to knowledge, the invention is the key to the betterment of society.

—Nelson Cheng

What ideas have I conceived to solve my existential problems?

CHAPTER 11

Adding Improvements to Inventions to Solve Problems

You Don't Have to Reinvent the Wheel

'It is not necessary to reinvent the wheel,' as an old saying goes. It is a waste of time reinventing the wheel, as the wheel can never be reinvented.

The biggest room in the world is the room for improvement.

—Helmut Schmidt

It is when we eliminate rules or boundaries in problem-solving that we achieve breakthroughs.

—Nelson Cheng

Revolutionary inventions ignore the rules.

—Nelson Cheng

The chapter lists some of the ground-breaking inventions developed through the efforts of others such as the radio, the elevator, the steam engine, the car, the telescope, the airplane, the light bulb, the television, and the cotton gin.

The Invention of the Radio

The 1890s saw Nikola Tesla and Marconi competing to develop radio technology. Many early patents went to Tesla. Heinrich Hertz had discovered electromagnetic radiation a decade earlier, which was capable of both transmitting and receiving radio waves. The discovery, however, had no practical application for him. All these technologies were combined by Marconi to create the radio, the first commercially available device of its kind.

Guglielmo Marconi radio

The Invention of the Elevator

As another example, the elevator was invented. People used mechanical devices to climb tall buildings in ancient Egypt. The Industrial Revolution and urban growth led to the construction of taller buildings, resulting in people having difficulty ascending and descending multiple flights of stairs. An elevator was invented that was powered by either steam or electric engines and pulled up by a rope.

Otis big brake invention

Ropes, however, tend to break. If the rope of an elevator broke and the carriage dropped, even if the elevator only went a few floors, you would suffer severe injuries, if not death.

Otis invented a safety brake that prevented an elevator from crashing when a rope snapped, and it was activated by a sudden fall. There was no longer a major danger posed by buildings taller than a few stories, causing skyscrapers to be built.

The Invention of the Steam Engine

Only steam engines were available almost sixty years before Watt's design. The first steam engine design was patent in 1698 by Thomas Savery for removing water from coal mines. After that, Thomas Newcomen improved the design, allowing it to work at atmospheric pressure, and the design became the industry standard for over fifty years.

Watt's major contribution was the development of a separate condenser, which enhanced the efficiency of the process.

James Watt and steam engine

The Invention of the Car

During a time when many people still travelled by horseback, Ford introduced the Model T in 1908. It was the first mass-market automobile to gain mass-market appeal and success.

In 1885, Karl Benz invented the first internal combustion engine, and many other engineers improved the design to improve efficiency, comfort, and performance over the next few decades.

This machine was manufactured more efficiently by Ford. By implementing an assembly line, he improved production efficiency and brought the cost of each unit down to a point where people could afford it.

Ford car assembly line

The Invention of the Airplane

Ever since humans first dreamed of flight, they have longed for it. People have wished to break free of gravity for thousands of years, from Leonardo da Vinci's sketches to the story of Icarus.

The Wright brothers were not the only ones of their time to try and build a machine capable of powered flight.

George Cayley was the first to go from designs with flapping wings to designs with fixed wings. Otto Lilienthal later used many of those designs to create gliders with fixed wings and test them, producing a wealth of data that would later be used by the Wright brothers.

In addition, the Wright brothers were able to make use of another recent invention of their day: the internal combustion engine from automobiles. Thankfully, they were alive when this technology first became available.

Their real innovation lay in the designs that allowed them to steer and control their planes. This is how history aeroplane is made.

The Transitional Model A of the Wright brothers

The Invention of the Telescope

The first telescope was not developed by Galileo but by a Dutchman called Hans Lippershey, who took advantage of the ever-improving capabilities of glassmaking to create devices that magnified.

Apparently, Galileo heard about these and recreated them in his own way, improving upon them even. Using these new optics for scientific purposes for the first time, he has contributed greatly to science.

Galileo is credited as the inventor of the telescope

The Invention of the Light Bulb

Thomas Edison

This invention may be the most famous in history, and its symbol is the essence of all ideas. The light bulb wasn't invented by Thomas Edison. Neither was the glass bulb or its glowing filament. In 1880, he simply improved the previous designs to Arc lamps, the first electric light devices, which were invented by Humphry Davy about seventy-eight years ago.

However, they didn't last long and were far too bright. Using carbonised paper as a filament, Joseph Swan invented the first light bulb in 1850. Unfortunately, his design did not work and was not durable or efficient, making them not commercially viable.

In subsequent experiments, Swan and Edison found better materials, and eventually their two companies merged to market their new improved design together, though most people only remember Edison.

The Invention of Television by Philo Farnsworth

Philo T. Farnsworth

TV pioneer Philo Taylor Farnsworth was an American inventor. Early electronic television owes a great deal to his contributions. In 1927, he invented the first fully functional all-electronic image pickup device, the video camera tube, the image dissector, and the first fully integrated all-electronic television system.

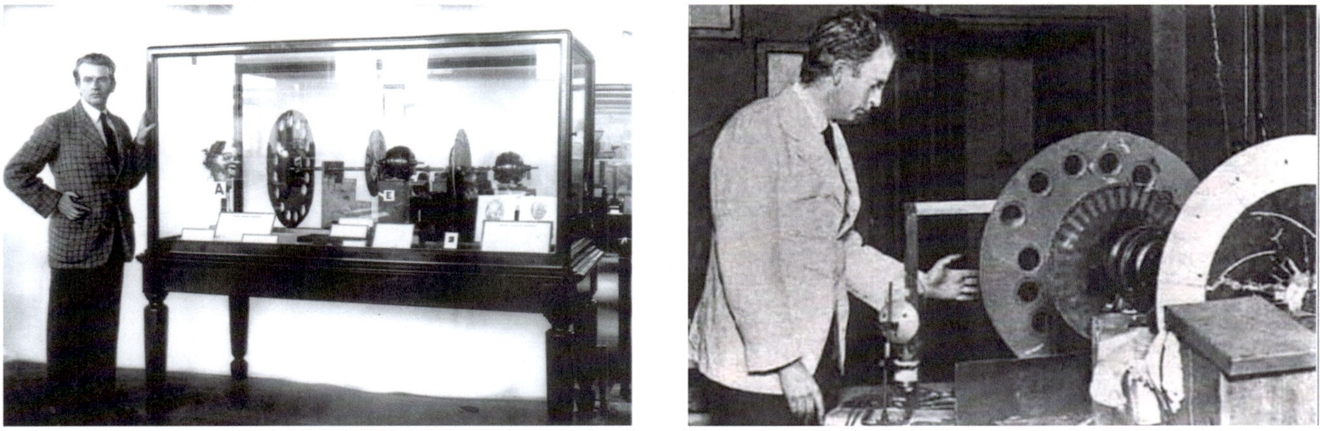

Baird Mechanical TV in 1926

A great example of his invention was only possible because of numerous other inventions across industries. He combined the development of the cathode ray tube (by Ferdinand Braun) with a way to scan images using electrons, something he apparently had been thinking about since he was in high school.

At the time, he also outperformed the mechanical TV technology that was competing with him.

The Invention of the Cotton Gin

In the United States, cotton was predominantly grown during slavery, and the fibres were short. At the time, machines that tried to separate seeds from fibres (roller gins) did not work well with this process, so much manual labour was required. As a result, the state of Georgia sponsored an engineering effort to develop a more efficient design. Wire teeth were placed on the rollers by Whitney to improve on the roller gins. Hence, cotton gin with teeth was invented.

The above inventions show that the progress of society is mainly the result of improvements in inventions around the world. The best companies don't believe in excellence—they believe in continuous improvement, as pursuing perfection can impede improvement.

You cannot hope to build a better world without improving the individuals. To that end, each of us must work for his own improvement and, at the same time, share a general responsibility for all humanity, our duty being to aid those to whom we think we can be most useful.

—Marie Curie

What can I do to improve my products?

Which features can I improve in my current product?

CHAPTER 12

Characteristics of Inventors in Terms of Problem-Solving

Definition of Characteristics

Characteristics can be defined as a distinguishing trait, the quality belonging typically to a person or group. It describes the individual peculiar, distinctive mean indicating a special quality or identity. It is a distinctive attribute that marks an individual or group out from others. It refers to a special quality, distinctive aspect of an individual or group. As we can see from the definitions, it is essential that we understand the characteristics they possessed to strive to cultivate them.

You become who you are by what you do.

—Nelson Cheng

Characteristics of an Inventor

Extremely Observant

Inventions are often the result of extraordinary observation. The hook-and-loop fastener system known as Velcro was developed in the 1940s by Swiss engineer George de Mestral after seeing tiny hooks on burrs attached to his hunting jacket.

Who you are is formed by what you do.

—Nelson Cheng

Persistence

The characteristic of persistence is probably one of the most admirable attributes of an inventor. A person with this trait could persist despite setbacks to achieve something. Even though it may be difficult or opposed by others, the inventor can do it or keep at it if he or she has this quality

Persistence is essential to growing as a person, otherwise it will be impossible.

—Nelson Cheng

Perseverance

A common personality trait among inventors is perseverance, which helps them overcome obstacles. Having perseverance means that when a challenge is facing them, they use both their mind and body to overcome it.

The inventor's perseverance gives them the ability to keep going even when they want to give up. They wouldn't have learned anything without perseverance and might make the next lesson even more challenging. By persevering through challenges, they can prevent a more difficult outcome later if they put the effort and time into the challenge when it is required.

It's not that I'm so smart, it's just that I stay with problems longer.

—Albert Einstein

Focus

Focus is another characteristic of an inventor. To stay on course, their centre of attention or activity focuses only on the subject they are currently involved.

Focus refers to the point at which rays of light refracted by a lens converge. In scientific Latin of the seventeenth century, the word means 'hearth, fireplace'. When sunlight is magnified, it can produce enough heat to ignite paper, so the metaphor of fireplace is quite appropriate to describe their convergence point. The concept of centre of activity has been derived from this sense of focus.

Focus is simply to do whatever you do passionately.

—Nelson Cheng

Never Stop Trying

An inventor's other trait is that they never stop trying. It is people who never gave up when there seemed no hope at all that have accomplished the most significant things in this world.

Great things happen to those who keep trying.

—Nelson Cheng

Never Stop Questioning

Another characteristic of an inventor is their curious mind; they never stop asking questions. Curiosity has its own reason for existing. Awe overtakes them as they contemplate the wonders of this universe. Every day, one need only try to comprehend a little more of this mystery.

Albert Einstein once said, 'The important thing is not to stop questioning. Curiosity has its own reason for existing.'

Why and 'How' are two essential words that we need to use as frequently as possible to solve problems.

—Nelson Cheng

Two vital words are 'Why' and 'How' whenever possible, use them to solve problems.

—Nelson Cheng

The two most significant words to remember are 'Why' and 'How' to solve problems using them if possible.

—Nelson Cheng

Overcoming the Fear of Failure

The brave man is not he who does not feel afraid, but he who conquers that fear.

—Nelson Mandela

Nothing in life is to be feared. It is only to be understood.

—*Marie Curie*

A crucial characteristic of inventors is their ability to overcome their fears of failure. Most people are affected by the fear of failure. Often, it paralyses them and prevents them from even trying.

Would it be different if I told you that failure is a good thing? Do you believe you should embrace failure instead of being afraid of it? Allow me to share as follows:

You can learn a great deal from failure.

Henry Ford once said, 'The only real mistake is the one from which we learn nothing.'

Our education prepares us for the world and all its challenges. We prepare ourselves for our respective careers by establishing the conditions for success. Increasing our expertise in our chosen fields progressively involves higher levels of learning.

Until we put our knowledge to work in the real world, in real-life situations, everything remains theoretical. It is then that failure takes on a whole new meaning. Each day at work is a competition.

For promotion, you are competing with everyone else who has a nine-to-five job. Entrepreneurs compete for market share. Naturally, we are upset and frustrated whenever we fail. However, failure represents a flaw in our performance or execution.

Failure is nothing but a representation of a fault in our performance or execution.

—Nelson Cheng

Which of the above characteristics do I still lack?

How should I develop those traits?

CHAPTER 13
Vision Is Realised through Invention

Most Inventions Started with a Vision

Helen Keller once said, 'The most pathetic person in the world is someone who has sight but no vision.' The statement is indeed a sad maxim when someone has sight but no vision in life.

Create your own vision to make your dreams a reality.

—Nelson Cheng

How Can a Vision Be Defined?

To see the future, you need vision.

—Nelson Cheng

In essence, a vision is envisioning a future that you want. In other words, a vision is not simply a goal, but the embodiment of what we hope and dream for in a particular area. It's not what has already happened, but what may come. Having a clear vision is vital for invention success. Clarity is an essential tool for achieving success.

We have a clear sense of purpose when we have a vision. We have a bigger picture of our business or our lives than simply setting and achieving short-term goals and tackling problems as they arise. The creation of real results is based on real efforts to reflect visions driven by passion and dreams.

You've got to give yourself the freedom to dream—to use your imagination to see and feel what does not yet exist. A vision is not the same as goals or objectives; those come from the head. A vision comes from the heart.

—John Graham

There Are Three Important Reasons Why You Need a Vision

Vision Unifies

In creating a vision for a company, everyone in the organisation feels as though they belong to a broader whole by providing a focal point or common interest. It is not only more meaningful, but it also helps form a team that is organised, focused, and working together to contribute to the vision.

Vision unites people of the same interest and purpose together.

—Nelson Cheng

Interests cannot be separated, and purposes cannot be divided.

—Nelson Cheng

Vision Inspires

It is inspiring to create a vision that is powerful. Such a vision motivates everyone within an organisation. The energy and enthusiasm generate lead to increased commitment and growth. Having a clear vision is especially important when things are difficult and stressful since it produces persistence and keeps you motivated.

Vision inspires and helps us to overcome fears.

—Nelson Cheng

We overcome fears through vision.

—Nelson Cheng

Vision Provides a Focal Point

A clear vision gives a sense of purpose and direction to a business. Defining your short- and long-term goals and making decisions along the way will be guided by your vision.

A leader has the vision and conviction that a dream can be achieved.
He inspires the power and energy to get it done.

—Ralph Lauren

Defining Your Vision

Vision is seeing into your future.

—Nelson Cheng

We've outlined why having a vision is so important; now let's talk about how to define your own:

Don't let fear restrict your vision. Be positive. Stay focused on success no matter how difficult it seems. Having a vision grounded in fear will limit your results since you will end up focusing more on damage control than positive change.

A clear and defined vision overcomes doubts and fear.

—Nelson Cheng

Clear and defined visions eliminate doubts and fears.

—Nelson Cheng

A vision should be specific, not general. It should be specific and provide clarity and direction. Also, it must be expressed clearly for it to be understood, indicating a specific future.

Your life was meant to fulfil a specific purpose.

—Nelson Cheng

Aim high. Make it extraordinary. Motivation, inspiration, and a sense of commitment to it are what will make it worthwhile. Having a good vision sets a high bar for excellence and performance and pushes your business to grow.

By aiming higher than you think you can achieve more than you anticipate.

—Nelson Cheng

It is possible to achieve much more than you thought possible
when you aim higher than you thought.

—Nelson Cheng

Where do I see myself in five years?

What is my vision in life?

CHAPTER 14

The Necessity of Solving Life's Problems

Solving Lives or Problems of Society Is Essential

For us to be able to improve the quality of our lives or improve society's standard of living, we must address all the problems that we encounter. If we ignore any of our or society's existential problems by sweeping them under the rug, we will hinder either our progress or that of society. We must therefore understand the importance of problem-solving or the necessity of it.

—Nelson Cheng

Necessity the Mother of Invention

There is a popular saying that says, 'Necessity is the mother of invention.'

Many inventions have been created because inventors recognised inherent needs. Inventors often saw a need or necessity and discovered that they could create something to meet it.

There is always a solution to any problem or need that arises. Since the dawn of mankind, men have continuously evolved in problem-solving, offering solutions to every need arising from society.

For a solution to be found, we must be able to recognise a need or a problem as early as possible.

As the saying goes, 'Invention, it must be humbly admitted, does not consist in creating out of the void, but out of chaos' (Mary Shelly).

Meeting the Necessity of Life Leads to the Convenience of Life

It's easy for us to take the inventions of the past century for granted given our familiarity with them. Every morning, we wake up, turn on the lights, make some coffee, then turn on the TV to watch the news. Our e-mails and phone messages are checked; we get into our car and perhaps drive to the office. These conveniences are all relatively new in our world today, but we would never imagine living without them.

In the late 1800s, Wilbur and Orville Wright took the ideas that had been around for hundreds of years and created the first and only functional flying machine. As a result, people began to live closer together and goods and services were supplied across the globe. Prior to the invention of the airplane, men take days or months to travel to distant places before the invention of the airplane. Today, men can travel thousands of miles within hours since the invention of the airplane. Such is the convenience of the airplane.

Everyone's life is now influenced by computers and the internet. It is hard for anyone to imagine a world without instant access to the knowledge of the world by using the internet, and anyone who has written a book or done homework on a typewriter knows the value of the computer.

Smartphones have played a significant role in connecting the world, entertaining, and educating mankind. In the past, people were only able to learn about what was going on elsewhere through radio, television, and newspapers, which was the only way that they could keep up to date with world events. We rely on real-time news nowadays and take it for granted. We cannot imagine our lives without smartphones because they provide us with so much comfort and convenience.

Electricity is something we pretty much take for granted today. Many of the things we depend on in our daily lives aren't apparent until we lose power during a storm. Despite this, it has only been in practical use for a relatively short time in history. Edison and Tesla brought us the form of electricity we use today, even though the notion of electricity has been around for many years.

The advent of electricity has brought with it so many conveniences that without it, men would have to deal with all the inconveniences of heating their houses during winter and those living in the Middle East would find it to be unbearably hot during the summer without electricity to power air conditioners.

Henry Ford is one of the people who are responsible for the automobile and its creation. Even though Ford didn't invent the automobile, he did develop a method to produce cars at a price that was affordable to the average man. By introducing the automobile, mankind was liberated from their limited space to travel independently.

It would have never occurred to Alexander Graham Bell that this invention, designed for communication in local areas, would be as functional as it is today. The old wooden crank phone hanging on the wall of the kitchen has come a long way. The cell phone has become one of the most used technologies of our time, and we now carry one with us wherever we go.

We are constantly improving and advancing our technology, but without these essential inventions, nothing we do today would be possible.

Is there anything conceived that might aid in the solution of existential problems or improve quality of life while reading chapter 12?

What convenience will it offer society?

CHAPTER 15
Inventions Reflect the Evolution of Human Intelligence.

Human intelligence and imagination have no boundaries, so there is no limit to growth.

—Nelson Cheng

The evolution of human intelligence is reflected in inventions.

Humanity has been faced with many obstacles that are often unpredictable throughout history. People are likely to thrive when faced with such uncertainty if they adapt to a variety of environmental conditions.

The evolution of mankind is reflected in the timeline of historic inventions. This chapter contains a chronological list of technological inventions that are particularly significant or important.

In the Palaeolithic Age, men hunted and women gathered food using simple tools and living a nomadic lifestyle.

As mankind evolved, the Neolithic Age, or Stone Age, began. It was the Neolithic Revolution that led to the birth of agriculture, which took *Homo sapiens* from isolated groups of hunters and gatherers to farming villages and then on to technologically advanced societies with temples and towers

Stone was the preferred material for toolmaking during the Neolithic period, which lasted 8,400 years, although copper and arsenic bronze was developed by the end of this era.

The Bronze Age and the beginning of bronze-smelting coincides with the rise of the first cities and the advent of writing in the Ancient Near East and the Indus Valley. Bronze Age is viewed as a 2,000-year period that began in 3300 BC and ended in 1300 BC

About 1300–1175 BC, the Late Bronze Age collapses, destroying most Near Eastern cultures and weakening the rest. Indus Valley Civilisation collapses at the same time. The Iron Age begins at the same time. Even though the typical definition of the Iron Age varies region-to-region (e.g., 510 BC in Greece, 322 BC in India, 200 BC in China), we define it for the purposes of this article as ending in 510 BC.

Many Indian developments between AD 300 and 600 BC are uncertain because old documents (such as the Sushruta Samhita and Natyashastra) were edited without being documented specifically. During the Gupta dynasty (mid-3rd century AD), most of these texts were canonised.

From the fifth century BC until the twentieth century, mankind made numerous inventions as they evolved.

As men evolved, the inventions from 1960 onwards were too numerous for us to consider at this point, so we will focus on a few noteworthy ones. Listed below are several inventions ranked by their significance, importance, and use by year:

- The first working laser was created by inventor Theodore Maiman in 1960.
- The *Vostok* 1 completed the first crewed spaceflight in 1961.
- Herbert A. Gilbert created the first electronic cigarette in 1963. Often credited with its invention; Hon Lik developed and commercialised the modern electronic cigarette.
- The original 0 series Shinkansen train is from 1964. The first high-speed rail commercial passenger service, it reached 210 km/h (130 mph) in 1964.
- In 1965, Stephanie Kwolek at DuPont invented Kevlar.
- Through UCLA, SRI, UCSB, and the University of Utah, ARPANET was deployed for the first time in 1969.
- In 1970, Japan invented the pocket calculator.
- Ray Tomlinson invented email in 1971.
- In 1971, Intel introduced the 4004 microprocessors, the first single-chip processor. The technology was developed by Federico Faggin using his silicon gate MOS technology. Through this, the personal computer (PC) was born.
- Salyut 1, the first space station launched by the Soviet Union, was launched in 1971.
- In 1972, the first video game console used primarily for playing video games on a TV was Magnavox Odyssey, designed and led by Ralph H. Baer at Sanders Associates.
- In 1973, Optelecom delivered the first fibre-optic communications systems to the US armed forces.
- In 1973, Xerox Alto introduced the first commercial graphical user interface. The Apple Lisa and the Xerox Star popularised the modern GUI.
- CERN developed the first capacitive touchscreen in 1973.
- Vinton Cerf and Robert E. Kahn proposed the Internet protocol suite (TCP/IP) for DARPA's ARPANET in 1973–74, thus creating the basis for the modern Internet.
- The Altair 8800 ignited the microcomputer revolution in 1975.
- A new DNA sequencing method was invented by Dr Walter Gilbert and Frederick Sanger in 1977, for which they were awarded the Nobel Prize.
- The first self-driving vehicle without rails or wires under the road was developed by the Tsukuba Mechanical Engineering Laboratory in Japan in 1977.
- The Global Positioning System (GPS) entered service in 1978. Despite not being the first, it was the first to be widely used by the civilian sector.
- In 1979, Microvision, the first handheld game console with interchangeable game cartridges, was released.

- Fujio Masuoka, working for Toshiba, invented flash memory (both NAND and NOR types) in 1980. Flash memory was introduced to the public in 1984.
- Test flights were conducted in 1981 to prepare for full operation of the space shuttle in 1982.
- CD-ROMs were used to store and play music, but not to write data. They were introduced in 1982.
- In 1982, the Epson HX-20, a portable laptop computer with 8/16-bit capability, was released.
- Stereolithography was invented by Chuck Hull in 1983.
- Motorola created the Dyna TAC 8000X, the first commercially available cell phone, in 1984.
- In 1985, Yellow Book standard developed by Sony and Philips adapted the format to hold any form of binary data.
- John B. Goodenough, Rachid Yazami, and Akira Yoshino invented the lithium-ion battery in 1985. Since then, modern consumer electronics and electric vehicles have been powered by lithium-ion batteries.
- Sir Tim Berners-Lee, an English engineer, and computer scientist introduced the World Wide Web to the public in 1990.
- SanDisk introduced the first commercial solid-state drive based on flash memory.
- Mosaic, the first popular web browser, was released in 1993
- IBM Simon, the world's first smartphone, was introduced in 1994.
- Ericsson Mobile developed the first generation of Bluetooth in 1994. This is a technology that allows electronic devices to communicate over short distances.
- Philips, Sony, Toshiba, and Panasonic invented and developed DVDs in 1995. Despite having the same dimensions as compact discs, DVDs offer higher storage capacity than Compact Discs while having the same dimensions.
- Ciena and Sprint deployed the first commercial wave division multiplexing system in 1996. It provided the internet with its massive capacity.
- SaeHan Information Systems released the first portable MP3 player in 1998.

Inventions of Twenty-First Century

- During the year 2000, Sony developed the first prototypes of the Blu-ray optical disc format. A prototype player was released in 2004.
- The original iPhone was released by Apple in 2007. Even though it wasn't the first smartphone, it popularised the touchscreen format.
- The first blockchain was created by Satoshi Nakamoto in 2008.
- A Japanese solar sail spacecraft, *IKAROS*, was launched in 2010.
- In 2010, the first synthetic organism, Mycoplasma laboratory was established by the J. Craig Venter Institute.
- The first prototype of an extreme ultraviolet lithography machine was released by ASML in 2010
- It was the first integrated quantum computing system for commercial use launched by IBM in 2019.
- Pfizer and BioNTech developed the first RNA vaccine for Covid-19, gaining approval from the FDA in 2020.

Inventions such as the ones outlined above reveal that human knowledge increases, and this increases inventions, which are the reflection of human intelligence's evolution.

In the last three decades, I have heard that technological advancements, advances in knowledge, and increased travel represent sure signs of an end time. Just look at the staggering advances in computing power, and you'd be forced to conclude that technology and knowledge are rapidly expanding.

A biblical prophecy that talks about knowledge increasing in the end times can be found in Daniel 12:4: 'But you, Daniel, keep this prophecy a secret; seal up the book until the time of the end, when many will rush here and there, and knowledge will increase.'

The creative power of the human mind has no limits, and that's why it can grow indefinitely.

—Nelson Cheng

In what way am I benefited by the listed inventions?

Are there improvements I can make to the listed inventions?

CHAPTER 16
Why Is Invention Necessary?

Problems Need to Be Solved

A problem can't be solved unless the right questions are asked.

—Nelson Cheng

Asking the right questions is key to solving a problem.

—Nelson Cheng

The purpose of an invention is to solve a particular problem using technology. It is through an invention's technical features that it solves a problem—the purpose for which it was invented. A patent requires the use of the laws of nature to achieve the technical character.

Society Needs to Progress

Progress is directly correlated to inventions in any society.

—Nelson Cheng

Technological progress and human progress rely heavily on inventions. The invention of new gadgets has greatly improved our lives. Think of what your life would be like without a fridge or washing machine, for example. You would have a hard time storing certain foods at home and doing the dishes by hand. It became easier to live after these products were developed and distributed.

Society has benefited significantly from inventions such as new tools, devices, processes, and medicines. A wide array of inventions is helping people around the world live longer, healthier, and more productive lives and providing new ways to build, move, communicate, heal, learn, and play.

The speed of progress in any society is directly proportional to that of its inventions.
—Nelson Cheng

Existing Technologies Need to Improve

The invention makes it possible to improve on the existing technology. More changes and innovations are possible in the contemporary world. It is possible to learn more about famous people thanks to inventions than we do today. Inventors who do this do so in a way that benefits the entire world. As a fundamental principle, inventions are made to serve a function. Nothing has ever been invented for destructive purposes, except military weapons.

There are no constraints on the human mind, no walls around the human spirit, no barriers to our progress except those we ourselves erect.

—Ronald Regan

Society Relies on Inventions to Solve Major Challenges

An example of this nascent challenge is the current coronavirus pandemic. In response to the current crisis, mRNA vaccines, antigen rapid tests (ARTs), and polymerase chain reaction (PCR) test kits have been developed at unprecedented speed. The writer and a member of the Magna Think Tank developed disinfectants for facial masks and surgical gowns to help protect healthcare workers during the early outbreak of the Covid-19 pandemic. Details of his invention will be covered in other chapters of this book.

Inventions transformed yesterday's challenges into today's norms.

—Nelson Cheng

New Inventions Generate Revenue during Economic Downturns

According to People's Vaccine Alliance statistics, Pfizer, BioNTech, and Moderna, three of the most successful Covid-19 vaccine suppliers, each earn $65,000 in profits every minute. During the annual STAT summit, which takes place from 16 to 18 November, CEOs of the pharmaceutical sector released numbers based on the latest reports.

The Alliance estimates that Pfizer, BioNTech, and Moderna will make $34 billion in profits this year between them. This is more than $1,000 a second, $65,000 a minute, or $93.5 million a day. During the pandemic, these companies created five new billionaires, with a combined net worth of $35.1 billion.

Why Were PCR Test Kits Developed?

In the wake of Covid-19's global spread, a test kit was urgently needed to test for infection and isolate infected individuals. The result has been the development of PCR test kits for the diagnosis of the Covid-19 in January 2020.

PCR stands for a polymerase chain reaction. It is a test that detects the genetic material of an organism, such as a virus. If you have the virus at the time of the test, the test detects its presence. Even after the virus is no longer active, fragments of the virus can be detected.

Since February 2020, the PCR test has been the gold standard for diagnosing Covid-19. Results are reliable and accurate.

Why Were Antigen Rapid Test Kits Developed?

It takes several hours for the results of a PCR test to be analysed in the laboratory. Depending on the workload of the laboratory, it may take up to two days in most countries.

For real-time updates of infection, a faster test method was needed. It was necessary to develop simple and easy-to-use self-testing kits for Covid-19 infections to ease the burden on healthcare workers. Accordingly, the antigen rapid test was created. The results can be obtained within fifteen minutes with high accuracy and are safe for children (if an adult is present).

In addition to being safe, easy, convenient, and most importantly, ART kits are a vital component in keeping us and our loved ones safe. Our health is monitored by a rapid antigen test that gives us peace of mind. Hence the invention of the antigen reaction test (ART) kit.

Inventions are necessary to solve problems, as shown by the examples above.

Invention, it must be humbly admitted, does not consist in creating out of void but out of chaos.

—Mary Shelly

Is there any way for me to solve my existential problem?

CHAPTER 17
A Guide to the Invention Process

The progress of life is not a state of being, but rather a process.

—Nelson Cheng

The revolutionary invention is about ignoring the rules.

—Nelson Cheng

Invention Process

It comprises steps for seeing a problem, conceptualising a solution, and implementing that solution.

Seeing a Problem

It is common for inventions to solve a specific problem. When coming up with a great idea, brainstorm the problem you are trying to solve. During the process of documenting your invention, you will need to write down all your thoughts. When you come up with an idea you think could work, develop it by laying out exactly what it should consist of. Then, lay out exactly how it will be manufactured and marketed.

Your invention is protected at a fundamental level by a record of your invention. You should keep all your notes in a journal, which a witness should sign and date. As soon as you have developed your invention, take steps to protect its confidentiality until you have obtained a patent, a process that can take up to three years. Witnesses and third parties with knowledge of the invention should sign confidentiality agreements. If a third party discloses details about your invention to others, you can sue for damages.

Whatever the problem, be part of the solution. Don't just sit around raising questions and pointing out obstacles.

—Tina Fey

Conceptualisation of a Solution

The concept of conceptualisation is the development of ideas for the most optimal solution to the design problem. It is essential that these ideas come directly from the product idea and the stated definition of the design problem. Product ideas tend to spring from a need or desire, often expressed in non-specific terms, expressed by people as a desired outcome.

We look solely at conceptualisation solutions only. The principal components are simplicity, support, familiarity, encouragement, and safety. The discussion then moves on to the more basic tools for conceptualising designs. Among them are creativity tools, brainstorming, decision-making, and concept optimisation.

Every problem has a solution. You just have to be creative enough to find it.

—Travis Kalanick

Implementation of a Solution

A problem will only be solved through implementation, which requires careful attention to detail. Here are the three main steps: developing a solution and preparing to implement it, monitoring, and implementing the action, performing a review and analysis of the success of the action.

Preparation and planning must be thorough according to the severity of the problem, or the complexity of the solutions required. Planning and preparation involve the following main elements: creating an action plan. The actions to be taken implement a schedule, resource requirements, containment of adverse consequences, action management, planning a review, and making sure those involved are selected, briefed, and trained. The details for the plan of action for implementing a solution are outlined in the next chapter.

If you define the problem correctly, you almost have the solution.

—Steve Jobs

If the challenge exists, so must the solution.

—Rona Mlnarik

Did I see any problems that needed to be solved?

CHAPTER 18

A Plan of Action for Implementing a Solution during Problem-Solving

I truly believe there's always a solution to every problem.

—Maira Kalman

What Is a Solution?

An answer or explanation for an issue that has troubled you. A solution is defined as a method for dealing with a problem or a solution to a difficult situation.

Implementing a solution involves determining which actions are needed and how they will be accomplished. If the problem is not simple or routine, then a detailed action plan is essential. A detailed action plan must identify and record the following components:

The Plan of Actions

To achieve the expected results, these must be identified fully and precisely. Identifying the expected outcomes of these actions will help you determine when they are successful.

A plan without action is a worthless plan.

—Nelson Cheng

State Your Objective

To reach a goal, rank the individual goals based on their importance.

List the actions needed to achieve each goal, determine the sequence in which they should be carried out, and record them.

Add details to the plan that describe what a successful outcome will look like for each action.

Organising the Actions

You create a schedule of the actions by first identifying the amount of time required to complete each task. You can calculate how long it will take to reach the objective by representing this information on the diagram, and calculating when each action will begin and end, based on the starting time. Charts showing the sequence and duration of actions can be used to represent simple plans.

Chain diagrams and flow charts are more appropriate for complex plans. Organising your actions with diagrams can help you use time and other resources more efficiently. For example, when creating a schedule. You shouldn't be overly optimistic in your time allocations for each action. For tasks that must be completed on time or that are susceptible to delays, extra time is needed to accommodate delays and unforeseen obstacles.

Resource Requirements

Defining the resources necessary for each action requires precise definitions, including their type, amount, and timing. Resources must be defined separately. In some situations, time is an invaluable resource that is sometimes overlooked. The type of questions that should be answered will determine the kind of resource.

Contingency Plans for Adverse Consequences

They must be incorporated into the plan. When constructing and evaluating your solution, you have considered the potential side effects and made corrections to minimise them. However, you must identify everything that could turn out wrong during implementation and devise countermeasures. It includes even minor issues such as a sick key person. In a similar fashion to how risks are evaluated and minimised for solutions, the steps involved are quite detailed.

Controlling the Action

The implementation must be monitored and controlled unless the solution is very simple or routine. As a result, this approach is an effective way to lead and manage the manpower, to measure their progress at specific intervals, and to take corrective action if deviations from the plan occur.

To manage the implementation, follow these steps:

Determine which actions require supervision and monitoring after completion (e.g., where the person has no previous experience with the required actions).

At what stage should progress be measured (e.g., upon completion of specific objectives or major activities; at critical stages)?

In what ways should results have been achieved by this point in the process?

Provide details about the actual results and who will be measuring them.

Plan for correcting variances between expected and actual results.

Does the plan need to be reviewed?

Finally, you must check the plan to ensure that to achieve the goals and the overall goal, the actions listed will be taken. You can accommodate unexpected delays with your time schedule. Do the resources you estimate accurate? It will be possible to keep the action on track with a management plan for controlling the action.

Lack of planning equals futile results.

—Nelson Cheng

What did I learn from chapter 16?

CHAPTER 19

A Country's Progress Is Enhanced by Solving Problems through Inventions

It Is the Inventions of the Country that Lead to Its Progress

Like John F. Kennedy, thirty-fifth president of the United States once said, 'Those who came before us made certain that this country rode the first waves of the industrial revolution, the first waves of modern invention, and the first wave of nuclear power. And this generation does not intend to founder in the backwash of the coming age of space. We mean to be part of it—we mean to lead it.'

In current times, and perhaps throughout human history, the United States of America is the most powerful country in the world. The tremendous advantages of scientific research and inventions in the United States further indicate the nation's technological and economic leadership over other countries. They are also examples of innovation more generally.

The fact that the US has won more Nobel Prizes than any other country since the award's inception in 1901 is another testament to the nation's inventions propelling its economic and technological progress. Since 1901, the US has never lost its Nobel lead. In the United States, there are 371 Nobel laureates, mainly in the sciences, despite accounting for only 4 per cent of the world's population. There are many factors that contribute to this, including wealth, culture, and the economy, which encourage innovation and education. It also has a political culture that has long been attractive to highly educated migrants. The US has an advantage there due to all those factors, not just Nobel Prizes. However, the sheer number of US laureates is one way to measure it.

Innovations and Inventions Are Drivers of Growth for a Developing Country

Progress in life isn't a state of being, but a process.

—Nelson Cheng

Eight hundred fifty million Chinese people have been lifted out of poverty by China during one of the world's longest periods of sustained growth. This growth was made possible by investing in infrastructure and expanding its economy.

International trade and investment were also significant factors. It was typically gradual, pragmatic, and experimental in nature, relying on local pilot programs before expanding policies to other areas. China transformed itself from an agricultural economy based primarily on farming to an industrialised manufacturing hub. It is now the second-largest economy in the world. China is now at a crossroads in its development.

Four decades of reform and opening up have resulted in rapid industrialisation, urbanisation, and efficiency gains that can no longer sustain past growth rates. There is an urgent need to find new drivers of economic development due to declining returns on public investment, an aging population, and an unfavourable international environment.

This challenge is fully understood by China's leadership. For this reason, the Development Research Centre (DRC) of the State Council, the Ministry of Finance (MOF), and the World Bank Group (WBG) have conducted a joint research program on China's new growth drivers.

The DRC and WBG studied China's main challenges for more than two years and came up with a set of recommendations for policy and institutional reform. Team members worked together on topics such as economic growth and productivity, institutions, and government reform.

Among the top priorities are technology and innovation, human capital development and the labour market, entrepreneurship and competition, industrial upgrading, regional integration and development, global integration, and international competitiveness.

China's future growth prospects and development progress will be dependent on boosting productivity through innovation, and market competition will be the engine of productivity growth.

Technological Changes and Preparing for Their Impact

China's policymakers need to start preparing workers for the impacts of technology today. Adapting to emerging technology that impacts jobs, income, and income distribution may take time as it is developed and diffused but preparing for the future workplace must begin now.

Technological developments can create new job opportunities, but automation and artificial intelligence may deprive many workers of their current jobs or require them to learn new skills.

Skills are favoured by technological change, which can lead to income inequality as workers with more education and skills gain more advantages. Recent technological advances may further exacerbate inequity because they lead to 'winner takes all' outcomes. Routine jobs with medium skill levels, such as many in manufacturing, are especially vulnerable to automation.

A broad range of economies has seen the share of labour decline in recent years because of technological advances.

Innovating for a Digital Economy

While China has built a large and extensive national innovation system, there are still many ways in which it can be improved. By expanding R&D tax credits and other innovation support programs that are open to all industries, China's top-down approach to promoting innovation could be supplemented with a more bottom-up, market-oriented, and decentralised approach. By doing so, the country can avoid missing out on innovation outside its policy focus areas or miss identifying the industries and technologies of the future. R&D funding could be redirected more to the public sector.

The purpose of this research is to complement private R&D and to raise the share of R&D dedicated to basic research in China.

China could also expand global innovation partnerships and joint R&D projects so the government's promotion of 'indigenous' innovation doesn't lead to technologies that are applicable only in China.

Almost everybody today believes that nothing in economic history has ever moved as fast as, or had a greater impact than, the Information Revolution. But the Industrial Revolution moved at least as fast in the same time span and had probably an equal impact if not a greater one.

—Peter Drucker

To progress, what innovations does my country need?

Is there a way for me to contribute to my country's innovation?

CHAPTER 20

China's Inventions and Patents Will Soon Make It the World's Largest Economy.

Inventions and patents have become an important engine of economic growth.

In the 2006 annual report of the World Intellectual Property Organisation (WIPO), released, the international patents system appears to be emerging as a major engine of economic development, as reflected by an increase in filings.

Any country's advancement was largely due to its inventions, as this chapter confirms.

China's record number of inventions and patents filed is a strong indicator that it is on track to become the world's largest economy.

While WIPO's international intellectual property (IP) services, treaty adherence activity, and revenue base continued to grow in 2019, China surpassed the United States of America as the top source for international patent applications submitted to the Organisation.

In 2019, China filed 58,990 applications via WIPO's Patent Cooperation Treaty (PCT) System, surpassing the US (57,840 applications in 2019) as the biggest user of the PCT System, which helps incentivise and spread innovation—a position previously held by the US since the PCT began operating in 1978.

The World Intellectual Property Organisation (WIPO) reports in its World Intellectual Property Indicators 2020 report that China has led the world in the number of patent applications since 2011.

> The number of patent applications received by China's IP office in 2019 was 1.4 million, more than twice the number received by the second-busiest country, the United States (621,453). Japan (305,969), the Korean Intellectual Property Office (KIPO; 218,975), and the European Patent Office (EPO; 181,479) were the next largest patent offices. The five offices together represented 84.7% of the total worldwide. (World Intellectual Property Indicators Report: Trademark and Industrial Design Filing Activity Rose in 2019; Patent Applications Marked Rare Decline Geneva, December 7, 2020, PR/2020/871)

In China, we intend to acquire advanced technology, science, and management skills to serve our socialist production. And these things as such have no class character.

—Former Chinese president Deng Xiaoping

The former Chinese president realised the importance of acquiring advanced technology to help China progress. A country's rate of progress is directly proportional to its number of inventions and technological advancements.

China, the Richest Nation in the World

China has become the richest nation in the world thanks to so many inventions and patents filed. According to Bloomberg, McKinsey & Co ranked China as the world's wealthiest nation in its latest report.

According to the report, global wealth increased by threefold over the last two decades, but China essentially topped the list of the world's richest nations ahead of the United States.

In the ranking of richest countries in the world in 2021, China surpasses the United States as the wealthiest nation.

Rank	Country	Net Worth
1.	**China**	$113 trillion
2.	United States	$50 trillion
3.	Germany	$14 trillion
4.	France	$14 trillion

As of 2021, the United States owes China approximately $1.1 trillion. The Chinese economy reached the trillion-dollar mark in 2011, according to a US Federal Reserve report.

What should my country do to progress?

CHAPTER 21

Why Focus on Solutions When Solving Problems?

When the solution is simple, God is answering.

—Albert Einstein

What Is a Solution?

A solution is defined to solve a problem or overcome a difficult situation; the state of being solved: a particular instance or method for solving or explaining.

How to Develop a Solution?

Take Your Eyes off the Problem

Solution development begins with taking your eyes off the problem. Our society needs to relearn the art of resting and relaxing. The practice promotes mental clarity, enables us to solve problems creatively, and prevents many illnesses that arise from chronic tension and worrying.

Stay Positive

People with a positive attitude maintain a larger perspective and see the big picture, which enables them to come up with solutions, while those with a negative attitude maintain a narrow perspective and are more likely to focus on problems.

Spend More Time on the Solution

Concentrate 90 per cent of your energy on solutions and 10 per cent on problems. The problem should be identified, but never dwelled on it; concentrate on solutions instead.

Focusing on solutions rather than problems is more important than having a vision of success. Occasionally examine the problem to find the solution, as sometimes the solution lies inside of it. Spend 10 per cent of your time on problem-solving.

People continue to make something that looks cool but is difficult to make instead of finding solutions to actual human problems, which is why the robotics industry has been slow to develop. Focusing on technology can be costly if you don't know where to begin.

Develop a Simple and Effective Solution

Focus on solving human problems, rather than developing sophisticated technology.

The Power of Focus in the Development of the Solution

Being able to concentrate and avoid distractions especially in the digital age is absolutely essential to the development of your best solution.

—Nelson Cheng

Take a moment to consider it. Things that distract you are things that draw your attention away from what your attention should be/could be doing. You won't be able to focus on the work that requires uninterrupted time for deep thought, flow, play, introspection, and execution if your attention is elsewhere. In other words, the more you end up distracted over there, whether you plan it or not, the more your attention gets side-tracked and lost.

Focus is one of the most critical life skills in developing a solution to a problem. A person's ability to focus mentally is considered an important predictor of developing a solution. Along with intelligence and grade point average, it may be one of the most critical indicators. Despite our inability to increase intelligence, we can greatly enhance our ability to focus during the development of a solution.

Occasionally we find ourselves unable to attend to a task because we are simply distracted. No matter how hard we try, our minds tend to wander. Others start thinking about all the things they need to accomplish, while others start daydreaming.

It takes time and patience for one to improve their mental focus. The process of training one's concentration may be quite challenging at times. You might find it extremely helpful to keep a few inspirational foci quotes handy to help you stay motivated in these situations. We can also benefit greatly from reading the wise words of people who have been able to maintain a high level of focus throughout their lives.

People tend to underestimate the influence of well-chosen quotes from some of the wisest people. But once you peruse the following focus quotes, you'll quickly realise they're extremely helpful for overcoming mental sluggishness. You can quickly regain the necessary persistence and willpower to remain focused by reading these quotes and reflecting on their meaning.

I have selected a few of the most inspirational quotes about focus for your reading pleasure. Take these sayings to heart and follow them relentlessly during problem-solving.

The successful warrior is the average man, with laser-like focus.

—Bruce Lee

According to Bruce Lee, mental focus can make the difference between being average and extraordinary. He highlights the tremendous benefits of being able to reach the highest level of focus and concentration. But he also points out that if we can perfect our concentration skills, we can be so much more than just average.

I don't care how much power, brilliance or energy you have, if you don't harness it and focus it on a specific target and hold it there, you're never going to accomplish as much as your ability warrants.

—Zig Ziglar

The sun's rays can be used to burn something, but you need a burning glass to focus the light. The rays also need to be directed at a specific target. If not, nothing will ever catch fire. Achieving goals in life is the same.

Unfocused actions won't result in the desired results.

—Nelson Cheng

That's been one of my mantras—focus and simplicity. Simple can be harder than complex: You have to work hard to get your thinking clean to make it simple. But it's worth it in the end because once you get there, you can move mountains.

—Steve Jobs

Being highly focused is a challenging task. Focus requires time and effort, but as soon as you reach a certain point, you'll start experiencing powerful effects.

Instead of focusing on that circumstance that you cannot change—focus strongly and powerfully on the circumstances that you can.

—Joy Page

Don't worry about what you can't change. You'll end up wasting your time and decreasing your optimism. Put your energy towards the things that you can influence. When you do, you'll realise just how much more you can accomplish.

We cannot solve our problems with the same thinking we used when we created them.

—Albert Einstein

Lack of direction, not lack of time, is the problem. We all have twenty-four-hour days.

—Zig Ziglar

Living a focused life requires direction. All your actions can be guided by a clear goal if you have one. If you're not sure where to go, you'll wander aimlessly.

A life focused on direction is the key to success. Your actions will all be guided by your goals if you have a clear vision. Nonetheless, you will mindlessly wander around if you are unsure of where to go. In the same vein, our working hours are often less important than how we use them. The more we maintain a high level of focus, the more efficiently we can use the available hours of the day. Distractions, however, will deter us from completing much in the limited time we have available

We are what we repeatedly do. Excellence, then, is not an act but a habit.
—Will Durant

If you focus long enough on mastering a certain skill, you will one day be able to excel in this area. However, if you're not focused and switch from one random activity to another, it's unlikely that you'll ever master what you're doing. Instead, to persist with whatever we're doing until we excel in it.

Whenever you want to achieve something, keep your eyes open, concentrate and make sure you know exactly what it is you want. No one can hit their target with their eyes closed.
—Paulo Coelho

Make sure your life has a clear goal. You could waste valuable time if you spend it in an undirected and unfocused manner. Maintaining a higher level of focus and motivation will be easier when you know exactly what you want. In addition, it will give you the motivation to achieve your goals no matter what. If you don't have a dream or vision that drives all your actions, you are more likely to give up when things get tough.

It is during our darkest moments that we must focus to see the light.
—Aristotle Onassis

Each of us suffers and experiences misery from time to time. When faced with such challenging situations, it's extremely difficult to maintain a positive attitude. When faced with pain and suffering, our minds tend to focus only on the negative aspects of what has happened. The pain and suffering is overwhelming, and we wish it had never happened. The light is hard to see, especially during our darkest hours. Considering this, it is all the more important to trust that one day we will be able to draw important lessons from our experiences. In these challenging times, however, we should not lose faith or give up. It's more important to make the most of our remaining power to endure suffering.

Concentrate all your thoughts upon the work at hand. The sun's rays do not burn until brought to a focus.
—Alexander Graham Bell

We can achieve true greatness only when we are able to focus 100 per cent of our attention on the task at hand. It is likely that the output of our work will be affected if distractions interrupt our workflow. However, if you focus intensely on the work at hand, you'll be able to realise your full potential. Focusing your work will produce dramatic improvements in your results, just as the sun's rays ignite paper when focused.

Most people have no idea of the giant capacity we can immediately command when we focus all of our resources on mastering a single area of our lives.

—Tony Robbins

Distractions interfere with our ability to focus all our attention on one thing. Our great ability to achieve a great deal depends on our ability to overcome distractions. Focusing on one aspect at a time without letting distractions take our attention away is all we need to do.

How must I do increase the power of my focus?

CHAPTER 22

Avoid Blaming the World during Problem-Solving

Solutions are the only way to resolve problems, not blaming.

—Nelson Cheng

Fix the Problem Instead of Blaming

While solving a problem, never place blame for a problem; fix it instead. The problem will only be resolved when solutions are sought. It is important to take note to fix the problem, not blame. Problems cannot be solved by blaming them.

Victims are people who blame themselves or others for some error or problem. A person or thing is blamed when it is held accountable for a mistake or wrongdoing. In other words, we want others to be held responsible. Putting people on the defensive does not solve problems; it usually aggravates them.

In essence, blame is debasing one's self-respect by transferring one's negative actions onto others to reinforce one's view of self-worth as decent, right, and approved.

Instead of Blaming Others, Inspire Them

As you solve problems, you should inspire others, never blame anyone.

—Nelson Cheng

Those who want to inspire people should avoid blaming. Put your attention on solving the problem, not blaming. It is not good to blame, it is good to look for a solution.

Humans naturally blame others when something goes wrong. It happens on all scales.

Moving Beyond Blame

Developing more realistic and helpful narratives to overcome bias. We can improve our ability to learn better if we go beyond blame and work to overcome it. Building more just and humane learning organisations can be achieved by moving beyond blame

Remove the Culture of Blame

We live in the blame culture in our society. Rather than taking responsibility for their mistakes and fixing it, they blame anyone or anything for them. This culture needs to be removed for us to solve problems efficiently and speedily.

Put your energy into fixing the problem, not into blaming.

—Nelson Cheng

Remove the Blame Game during Problem-Solving

We shouldn't waste our time on the blame game. Don't waste energy trying to fix blame when you should be fixing the problem. By blaming, we surrender control in providing a solution.

The exercise of blaming is pointless. No matter how many faults you find in someone, and how much blame you place on them, it will not change your character. You only benefit from blaming when you are looking for external reasons for your unhappiness or frustration. If you blame another for something, you may succeed in making him feel guilty, but you will not succeed in changing anything about you that makes you unhappy.

There is no benefit in blaming. We will not be able to change anything in our lives until we admit to ourselves how we really feel.

Remove All Excuses during Problem-Solving

Blaming others is excusing yourself, it is important to realise that we cannot excuse ourselves by blaming others.

Taking responsibility for one's actions is everyone's responsibility. If you blame the world for your problems, you will get nowhere.

It's your responsibility to take responsibility when you make a mistake. Don't give up; acknowledge the mistake and take the blame. Passing the blame onto your team for a bad mistake you made is the worst thing you can do.

Learn from Our Mistakes during Problem-Solving

The misattribution of blame contributes to the repetition of mistakes. We learn so little from experience because we often point the finger at the wrong source.

It is not uncommon for mistakes to be repeated due to incorrect attribution of blame. Our failure to learn from experience often stems from pointing the finger at the wrong person.

It's always the blameless people who irritate me the most.

—Nelson Cheng

What must I do in order not to blame others during problem-solving?

CHAPTER 23

China, the Awakened Giant, Has Much to Teach Us in Problem-Solving

Let China sleep, for when she wakes, she will shake the world.

—Napoleon Bonaparte

China was once referred to by Napoleon Bonaparte as a sleeping giant two hundred years ago.

Until recently, the potential was not so obvious, and the challenge posed by this country was less apparent, but the sleeping giant has awoken and is now competing with the world. China has enjoyed an annual GDP increase of more than 2,000 per cent since Mao's death in 1976, a feat no other country has been able to match. The military divisions of the government have grown by 12 per cent annually (water, land, and air).

The giant has awoken: The United States has never viewed China as a threat before. As a result, the United States of America viewed China as a source of cheap labour, better laws, and vast land that was free from the heavy regulations of Congress. As a result, many companies have invested heavily, the ten largest being from car, airplane, shoe, and most technological companies. China's importance to the international community is evident due to the United States' view of it as a major investment hub.

Various economic tremors are being caused across the globe as a result of this awakened giant, building infrastructures such as the belt and road, connecting Asia with roads and rail services, and building infrastructures in developing countries at an unprecedented pace.

This awakened giant is the only country capable of ending the hegemony of the United States after the collapse of the Soviet Union. This awakened giant will become the largest economy in the world within the next few years and will be the only country capable of challenging the global order in history.

Its socialist market economy and communist ideologies have seen China transcend the ethos of being a communist country. Communism's state capitalism regulates and guides macroeconomics in accordance with market forces. The shift in global capitalism reflects this shift in economic and political models.

Western countries have responded to the challenge by banning Huawei's phone manufacturing, blacklisting in 2020, and imposing tariffs again. Several economic reasons justify these reactions, as China, if left unchecked, would likely cripple all American technology-based companies and dent the United States market.

This awoken giant plans to become self-sufficient by 2025 and have shaken the Chinese technology market. Companies are shifting out of the country, while new companies are being launched in China to replace the existing ones—a phenomenon marked by the launch of a new tech-driven stock exchange called STAR Market on the Shanghai Stock Exchange in July. One hundred twenty-four billionaires have been created thanks to its portfolio of twenty-five new tech companies.

Across seventy countries, Forbes found 2,755 billionaires in 2021—nearly a third more than the 2,095 listed in 2020. As with Forbes' previous World's Billionaires list, nearly half of individuals appear to be from the US and China. Since March 2020, China has gained 239 billionaires, bringing its total to 626.

A combined net worth of $2.5 trillion is held by China's billionaires, an increase of $1.3 trillion compared to last year. As a result of Hong Kong's 71 billionaires and Macao's one billionaire, greater China now has 698 billionaires, up from 456 last year.

The latest Forbes annual rich list says more billionaires live in Beijing than anywhere else in the world. The Business magazine reports that China's capital added 33 billionaires last year and now has 100 New York City, which hosted 99 for seven years in a row, was beaten by this feat.

Chinese technology firms and stock markets have helped it gain the top spot thanks to its quick containment of Covid-19.

In becoming self-reliant, China will challenge the existing order of political power in the world. It represents a challenge in investment and a challenge in technology advancement for the next century. According to Napoleon Bonaparte, the words of the French emperor have become reality. China has awoken, but people do not want to believe it.

What have I learned from the awakened giant, China?

CHAPTER 24

What Is the Significance of the Sleeping Giant in Me?

The only person you are destined to become is the person you decide to be.

—Ralph Waldo Emerson

There Is a Giant within Every One of Us

In the depths of each of us lie powers and abilities we never dreamed we possessed. If we aroused and harnessed those forces, we would revolutionise our life.

There are hidden potentials within you, undiscovered gifts, raw talents, innovations you've never imagined, songs you've never written, and discoveries of great value that divinity has engraved within man to impact the generations following you.

Your giant inside you is too big to be a dwarf. Your arms are too full to be mediocre. Your inner wealth is more valuable than the oil fields of Kuwait and the gold mines of South Africa combined.

In other words, you are endowed with immeasurable, unfathomable, and limitless power. As a result of these powers, the sleeping giant has been defined as the seed of greatness.

If a giant is asleep, it could be mistaken for dead if it is in a deep slumber.

—Nelson Cheng

The Giant Is Not Dead

The giant is not dead; the giant is only sleeping within you. If the giant arose, your life would be forever changed, and the sands of time would be permanently changed forever.

If the sleeping giant is awoken, then all humans will know for sure that a change has occurred, something is happening, and the system is being turned upside down and changing the order of things.

There is no greater loss of talent than an unfulfilled potential.

—Nelson Cheng

It is impossible to overstate the value of a potential unfulfilled.

—Nelson Cheng

When Should I Wake Up My Sleeping Giant?

Today is the day; it is the dawn of your new day, the brightest day of the year, and it is the time for your giant within you to rise to solve all your existential problems.

Your giant will make maximum impact in the season of change. You have broken the treatise and begun your journey towards greatness. Be the giant that you can be and impact the world positively for generations to come.

No matter your academic background or the level of education you have achieved, you will be outstanding in all your endeavours once your sleeping giant is awoken.

Henry Ford, the iconic owner of Ford Motors, didn't have any academic standing, but he turned out to be a genius in the automobile industry. Despite failing out of school, he learned to ride a bicycle instead.

Despite all odds, he became the pioneer of the mass assembly of cars at the age of forty. As one of the world's richest men at the age of sixty, he was one of the greatest of all time! Ford once said, *'Think you can or you can't, either way, you'll be right.'*

Among the greatest losses of talent is unfulfilled potential.

—Nelson Cheng

How the Giant in Us Can Be Awoken?

Believe in Yourself

A change of beliefs is the first step toward a personal breakthrough. What determines your fate is not your circumstances, but your belief and decision. Do not think lowly of yourself. There is a giant within you that just needs to be awakened. You can change the direction of your life at any moment when you wake up the giant within you in problem-solving.

What we are, depends on our beliefs and actions.

—Nelson Cheng

Change Yourself

You must change your inner world to change the world around you, hence the giant within you needs to be awakened. It is only through changing your inner world that you can change the world around you. What you do most of the time determines who you are. Most of the time, who you are is determined by your inner world.

Do Not Underestimate Your Potential

You have the potential of a giant within you. When it's awakened, you'll realise that whatever your mind conceives, it'll be able to achieve.

There is no man living who isn't capable of doing more than he thinks he can do.

—Henry Ford

Focus

Life provides us with whatever we focus on. If we keep focusing on what we do not want, we'll receive more of it. Creating any change begins with deciding what you want to accomplish so that you know what direction to move in.

A focused life will result in consistent thoughts.

—Nelson Cheng

Envision You're the One That Provides the Solution to Problem-Solving

If you talk about it, it's a dream; if you envision it, it's possible. You just need to you schedule it. Think about the possibility that you provide the solution to solving problems to wake up the giant of problem-solving within you.

There is nothing that can stop the giant from waking up within you except yourself.

—Nelson Cheng

Set a Dateline in Problem-Solving

A dream is a dream, a vision is a possibility, but a calendar is a real thing.

—Nelson Cheng

A vision is a possibility, but a calendar is a concrete reality. To track progress, we need datelines in everything we do.

A dream is a dream, a vision is a possibility, but a calendar is a real thing.

—Nelson Cheng

Conquer Your Fear

To discover our giant within, we must get over our fears. You should focus on what you want to achieve, rather than what you fear. Wisdom, strength, courage, passion, and everything else you need are already within you. By just contemplating how to solve the problem, you activate them.

Remember, We Exist to Solve Problems

We learn more from problems than without them. Your inner giant is there to help you solve problems. Life's greatest rewards are reserved for those who solve life's never-ending problems.

Solving problems enables you to get better, stronger, richer, quicker, or smarter. The talents you possess were put there by God for the betterment of humanity. Make a list of your problems, but focus your energy and power on solutions.

Solving life's never-ending problems offers the greatest rewards in life, as it pleases God.
—Nelson Cheng

It is the unfulfilled potential of talent that is among the greatest losses of talent.
—Nelson Cheng

What must I do to wake up my sleeping giant within me?

CHAPTER 25
The Importance of Adaptability Quotient in Problem-Solving

Adaptability is the key to our survivability.

—Nelson Cheng

Those who are able to best manage change are the ones who will survive, not the biggest or the smartest.

—Nelson Cheng

Problem-solvers need to know the importance of having high adaptability quotients by discarding obsolete ideas and embracing what is relevant to solving real-time problems.

—Nelson Cheng

What Is the Adaptability Quotient?

The adaptability quotient (AQ) is a measure of someone's ability to adapt. In a way, it's like IQ, which measures intelligence, or EQ, which measures emotional intelligence. This trait refers to the ability to identify what's relevant, to forget outdated knowledge, overcome challenges, and adapt to change in real-time. Your ability to adapt will determine your success in the future.

What Is the Importance of Adaptability?

Organisations must remain competitive by adapting and adjusting to changing customer demands, market trends, and technological advancements. Their leaders and employees must be able to adapt easily to rapidly changing situations to do this.

Unknowns are impossible to predict directly, but you can prepare for them. You will be more prepared to face whatever comes your way if you develop the skills to adapt to change and consider possible outcomes.

Almost all businesses were unprepared for a Covid-19 pandemic that spread across the globe in 2020. Business survival required quick decision-making, diverse solutions, and unlearning. Remote work was once thought to be impossible by companies, but a new perspective soon changed their minds.

Businesses that have been proactive in problem-solving, flexibility, innovation, and adoption of new technology have been the most prepared for an unprecedented year of change.

Companies that cannot adapt to new technologies quickly risk falling behind and losing market share. Technology that fails to catch on can also create consequences for companies that use it.

Change is a constant in our lives, those who are adaptable will be able to cope with whatever the future holds.

—Nelson Cheng

How to Develop Your Adaptability Quotient?

Acknowledge and Embrace Change

Whether you like it or not, change is inevitable. While you cannot prevent change, you can learn to embrace it and accept it.

A simple change in the workplace, such as an updated computer system or management adjustments, can send some people into a tailspin. You might resist the change and deny its existence, or you might become increasingly disengaged as things change.

Getting to a place of acceptance requires working your way through these phases. Find the positive in every new situation and accept change. Think of ways to turn upcoming changes into opportunities. How can you take advantage of them? If you want to move forward confidently, what problems do you need to overcome?

Ask Yourself Questions about Your Assumptions

Things that were once true won't always remain true. There are constant changes in life, so even though you think you know the best way to do something, it might not continue to be so. Changes in circumstances and new possibilities might lead to a new solution.

At any given time, adaptable individuals are ready to embrace a new solution and question their assumptions. Assess your processes on a regular basis. Can they be improved? Is there anything you haven't considered before? It is beneficial to receive constructive feedback from others to gain new insights on how to improve.

Take a Look at What the Future Could Hold

People who are adaptable understand that change is inevitable. Embracing this outlook allows you to be open to new possibilities. Consider the many possibilities that could impact your business or yourself in the future.

Would your work be completed by AI technology in the future? If so, how would you fit into that scenario? How can you ensure you don't fall behind when it comes to the skills and abilities that will be in demand in the years to come? Where do you see yourself in five years? A decade? Even twenty years from now?

The goal is not to guess the future or worry about everything that may go wrong. It's a way of preparing yourself for the changes the future will undoubtedly bring by visualising possible outcomes. Furthermore, it improves your imagination and creativity.

How to Develop Workplace Adaptability?

Workplace Flexibility Is a Must

The rigidity of an organisation sets it up for failure. Anything that does not bend breaks. You can adapt to crises more easily if you are flexible as an employer or manager. In addition, it will allow your employees to work the way they are most motivated, engaged, and productive.

Adjust the schedule, offer flexible hours, and allow working from home. Employees will find this an asset, and your business will benefit as well. Your business can maintain its operations despite unexpected emergencies if you have the flexibility to handle them.

Is your business able to operate remotely if there's a thunderstorm? Are employees able to work from home if a family member is sick? You are more likely to be able to deal with surprises and emergencies if you practice flexibility.

Employees Should Be Allowed to Fail

Despite the fact that failure is never the goal, it provides an excellent learning opportunity. Failing is an opportunity to learn, so allow your team to do the same. Punishing or scolding someone for making a mistake doesn't prevent future mistakes, it just discourages people from being honest when things do go wrong. Fear of punishment may also discourage people from expressing new ideas.

Develop a work environment where failure is embraced as a learning opportunity. Innovation, creativity, and trying new ways to work are impossible without being open to the possibility of failure. Anticipating errors may be daunting, but it's essential to avoid stagnation. You shouldn't let that next revolutionary idea pass you by because you're afraid of the consequences.

Maintain a Continuous Feedback Culture in the Workplace

In the workplace, feedback is often sporadic and random, and it is often viewed as something to be feared. How many of us have had managers who only provided feedback when they corrected us or addressed a problem?

A culture of continuous improvement is fostered by businesses that prioritise constructive feedback.

By giving and receiving feedback, we can gain new insight into our ability to adapt and improve. We stay open to learning how we can become better by not becoming set in our ways. A flexible approach to change will allow you to spend less time being stressed out as you face new challenges.

Change should not be viewed as a barrier but as an opportunity.

—Nelson Cheng

How can I stay relevant? What are the traits I need to acquire?

CHAPTER 26
The Importance of Adversity Quotient in Problem-Solving

Those who have faced adversity in life appreciate the compassion, gentleness, and deep caring actions of those who have shown them.

—Nelson Cheng

Beautiful people aren't born; they're created through adversity.

—Nelson Cheng

Adversity quotient is the sum of resilience, tenacity, and persistency.

—Nelson Cheng

Adversity can be defined as a challenge or obstacle that disrupts our lives. It could be a physical or mental challenge could cause by a traumatic event or injury or a broken relationship from a divorce. To effectively solve problems, you need a high adversity quotient.

What Is the Adversity Quotient?

The adversity quotient is a yardstick to measure how successful a person is at handling adversity in life. The ability to handle adversity well is what determines one's adversity quotient. Resilience, fortitude, tenacity, and persistence are just a few of the other names used to describe it.

Those with a high adversity quotient are hardy and will not wallow in self-pity even when life brings them hardships. Adversity does not easily discourage him. With the world experiencing tumultuous pandemic times, having an adversity quotient is more important than ever. People with high adversity quotient are unquestionably valuable assets for any organisation.

How to Develop an Adversity Quotient?

Adaptability

Adapting to changing conditions in the physical world is essential for the survival of all living things, from the smallest organism to the largest dinosaur.

In many workplaces, employees who refuse to adapt to drastic changes, such as sudden cost-cutting measures or heavier workloads, will leave. An individual with high adversity quotient stays regardless of the circumstances. No matter what challenges life brings him personally or professionally, he will not be crushed.

Adversity quotient is a function of adaptability.

—Nelson Cheng

Control Your Emotions

It is important to be able to control one's emotions when faced with adversity. In a situation where one's emotional control can make a situation worse than it already is, gaining emotional control is crucial. In addition, people who control their emotions are usually aware that adverse circumstances will only affect them temporarily.

Seek Help from Friends or Colleagues

High adversity quotient individuals typically have a strong social support system. By using this support system, the individual will be able to absorb shocks when faced with difficult situations. Additionally, a strong social support system can provide emotional support when one feels depressed.

Being Positive about Life

Positive thinking is characteristic of people with high adversity quotient. Instead of seeing the half-empty glass, they will see the half-full one. Even criticism will be viewed positively and constructively.

A person with a high adversity quotient will perceive adversity as something within their control, meaning that they feel like they can influence it in some way.

A person who has faith that they can achieve a certain outcome
despite dire circumstances is more likely to act.

—Nelson Cheng

Develop the Perception That Adversity Is Temporary

Perception of an adversity's temporary nature is closely related to high endurance because they hope the adversity will pass; they will more likely endure it.

Leadership and the Adversity Quotient

Adversity quotient is a factor that affects a person's health, happiness, and wealth. Age has no effect on the adversity quotient; research concluded that children with a high adversity quotient are not so different from the traits of resilient adults.

In times of great challenges to the organisation, adversity quotients in problem-solving will prove to be helpful. Generally, the higher a leader's adversity quotient, the more likely it is for him or her to succeed in a challenging situation. An organisation's most valuable assets are those who get back up quickly after losing.

CHAPTER 27
Why Invention Is Used in Problem-Solving?

Any invention is not created out of void but out of a need or an existential problem.
—Nelson Cheng

The purpose of any invention is not to fill a void but to solve an existential problem.
—Nelson Cheng

The invention determines the speed of humanity's progress.
—Nelson Cheng

The speed of advancement of humanity depends on the rate of invention.
—Nelson Cheng

What Is an Invention?

An invention is a method for solving a specific problem using technology. A technical feature of an invention is intended to solve the problem or to accomplish the purpose of the invention.

What Is the Purpose of an Invention?

The invention is intended to serve a purpose. Inventions are anything you can create to complete your task more efficiently or fulfil the purpose of your task.

The Importance of Inventions

Inventions Extends the Lifespan and the Quality of People

Modern life is influenced by inventions in every aspect. For instance, the toilet and modern plumbing helped to improve hygiene and reduce exposure to human waste, making cities cleaner and more desirable to live in. In addition to reducing the spread of disease, the modern bathroom has also led to an increase in the average life expectancy, which has led to an increase in the world's population five times in a century.

Thanks to inventions such as the refrigerator, the oven, running water, pots, and pans manufactured safely, pasteurised products, and even meat thermometers, we eat better and more safely.

Inventions Improve the Quality of Our Daily Lives

It is true that there are many inventions that have changed the lives of many people. Listed below are a few things that are important today and will be important tomorrow.

- **Penicillin.** A lot of infections were cured with penicillin, which was one of the first antibiotics. In 1928, Nobel Prize winner Alexander Fleming discovered it accidentally in a Petri dish. This group of antibiotics is used to treat a wide range of infections in humans without harming them. As a standard antibiotic, penicillin was mass-produced during World War II to treat venereal diseases in servicemen. It remains one of the most important discoveries in the field of healthcare. Despite its almost unintended nature, this invention over the years has saved many lives.
- **Internet.** Vinton Cerf developed the internet in 1973 with the support of the Advanced Research Projects Agency (ARPA) of the US Department of Defense. The network was designed initially to provide a network of communication between research labs and universities in the United States, but it expanded over time. It is considered by many to be the most important invention of the twentieth century (along with the World Wide Web). More than 25 million computers were connected to the internet in 180 countries in 1996. This huge number illustrates the early rise of the internet. It is rare that you will find a household without Internet access today.
- **World Wide Web.** Arthur Clarke predicted that one day satellites would bring accumulated knowledge of the world to our fingertips, combining telephone, photocopier, television, and computers. A CERN employee, Tom Berners Lee, made the invention nineteen years later in 1989. Web technologies have revolutionised many fields, including education, music, finance, reading, medicine, and dating. It may rank among the greatest inventions in history.
- **Telephone.** With a thread at each end of two cups, Alexander Graham Bell connected them together so that he could talk from one end and listen from the other. We all carry this attachment in our pockets or hands today due to another revolutionary invention that was built on the work of this first. In the field of business and communication, the telephone, which was later developed into a mobile phone, has been lifesaving for mankind.
  To this day, no other work has been able to extend audible speech from within a room and across the globe. Even more, significance has been added to mobile phones ever since they have been able to combine more and more functions like calculators, weather forecasts, and many others. Around 80 per cent of ten-year-olds in modern societies own a smartphone. The statistics show how widespread this technology has become.
- **Airplane.** In 1903, the Wright brothers invented and flew the first airplane. Throughout all world wars, airplanes proved decisive, and they remain vital in the transport of passengers today. The number of flights has significantly increased over the years except for the current pandemic that reduces the number of flights. This invention builds our futures and improves life.

- **Television.** The creation of modern television is generally attributed to two people: Vladimir K. Zworykin and Peter Farnsworth. Another great invention was the television, which evolved from mechanical to electronic to colour to digital to smart and now 3D versions. We spend three to four hours a day watching TV, which has a significant impact on our family and social lives. Television is so fundamental that one cannot imagine a world without it. Even though the internet is an important medium, many people still view television daily. The duration of TV viewing has remained the same. The average person watches about three hours of TV every day. There has been no decline in this number since the 1990s, showing the importance of this invention.

How can I develop a solution to my existential problem?

CHAPTER 28

Turning Problems into Opportunities Singapore's Case Study 01

Why did Singapore develop the Newater Technology?

'Every other policy has to bend at the knees for our water survival,' Lee Kuan Yew famously announced during a water event in Singapore in 2008.

Former secretary-general of United Nations Mr Ban Ki-moon praised the Newater Technology, calling it 'the Elixir of Life'.

The Singapore Water Story

Historical Background

The water agreement was signed in 1961 and 1962, which allowed Singapore to continue to obtain water from Johor until 2011 and 2061, respectively, and allowed the island to separate from Malaysia in 1965.

Prime Minister Lee was not at ease with these provisions, even though the constitution had been enshrined in it during the separation in 1965. A statement made by Malaysia's first prime minister, Tunku Abdul Rahman, that he might 'turn off the water supply' if Singapore did not do what he wanted underscores the importance of Singapore's self-sufficient water supply.

The Problem It Faced

Having limited catchment areas and using 400 million gallons of water every day—the amount of water required to fill 715 Olympic-sized swimming pools—Singapore is unlikely to be a leader in water sustainability.

The Factor That Aggravated the Problem

Water was used as a political weapon against Singapore. A statement made by Malaysia's first prime minister, Tunku Abdul Rahman, that he might 'turn off the water supply' if Singapore did not do what he wanted underscored the importance of Singapore's self-sufficient water supply.

The Quest for the Solution to Solve the Water Problem

As Singapore became independent, Prime Minister Lee challenged the Public Utilities Board (PUB) to become self-sufficient and to 'capture every drop of rain' that fell. The nation's civil servants and engineers worked diligently to clean up the country's polluted waterways and increase its catchment areas in the decades that followed.

Singapore engineers had the idea of turning sewage or wastewater into potable water in the 1970s. In 1974, PUB built a pilot plant but eventually shuttered it due to cost and technological considerations, but planners didn't lose sight of their goal.

Several decades of research and gruelling engineering work in Singapore culminated in a water reclamation process that involves microfiltration, reverse osmosis, and ultraviolet radiation, which is now known as Newater.

Turning the Water Scarcity Problem into an Opportunity to Become a Global Hydro Hub

The city-state is well-positioned to become self-sufficient for its water requirements by 2061—when current agreements with Malaysia that allow Singapore to import water from Malaysia will lapse—but it is also recognised as a 'global hydro hub', a centre for water expertise and business opportunities.

As a result, Singapore is also home to more than 100 water companies that provide solutions to a variety of water challenges in the region. According to the United States Center for Disease Control and Prevention, the city-state is one of only two countries in Southeast Asia with a safe water supply (the other is Brunei).

During the official launch of Newater in 2003, then prime minister Goh Chok Tong said that Singapore's 'diminishing reliance on Johor water' was a positive development.

When water cannot be used as a political weapon against Singapore, both countries can focus on 'mutually beneficial cooperation', said Goh, who succeeded Lee as prime minister in 1990.

A total of four Newater plants exist in Singapore today, with the latest and largest having been completed in 2010. The plants will provide 40 per cent of the island's water by 2020. In order to meet 55 per cent of future water demand, PUB plans to triple its Newater capacity by 2060.

On a 2012 trip to the Newater complex in Changi, United Nations secretary-general Ban Ki-moon praised the technology, calling it the 'elixir of life', and recommending Singapore's experience and know-how be shared with other countries facing water shortages.

Singapore made history in 2002 when its brand of high-quality recycled drinking water, Newater, was introduced to the nation during the National Day Parade by then prime minister Goh Chok Tong.

Lee Kuan Yew also proposed damming Singapore's Marina Channel to create a freshwater reservoir in the 1980s. Engineers in Singapore built the Marina Barrage. Marina Reservoir, the city's first urban reservoir, was officially unveiled in 2008 along with the structure. The project added 10,000 hectares to Singapore's catchment area—one-sixth the size of Singapore. As a result of the Marina Reservoir and two other new reservoirs, the city's catchment area increased from half to two-thirds of its land area.

Several engineering innovations went into the construction of the Barrage, which has also received worldwide recognition. It has won several awards, including the top prize at the American Academy of Environmental Engineers' 2009 Excellence in Environmental Engineering Competition.

Singapore's remaining water needs are met by desalination, a process of purifying seawater so it can be drinking water. It is also supplied by reservoirs, imported water, and Newater.

The country's consumption of 400 million gallons of water each day could be met by desalinated water today. Singapore plans to create a fourth national tap that can meet 25 per cent of future water needs by 2060, even as this demand is expected to nearly double.

The Lee Kuan Yew School of Public Policy's former dean Kishore Mahbubani wrote in the foreword to a book on Singapore's water journey 'that if anyone had told Singapore in 1965 that it could be self-sufficient in water within 50 years, they would have been laughed out of court'. 'This impossible goal is on its way to being realized,' he said, even as Singapore values its water agreement with Malaysia.

Singapore can meet its water needs independently by 2061, according to then-PUB CEO Chew Men Leong in an interview with Bloomberg.

According to Grace Fu, the minister of Environment and Water Resources, in her remarks on World Water Day, 'We owe it to Mr Lee today—for through 30, 40 years of hard work, research, development, we have come close to being self-sufficient in water.'

Singapore's first prime minister, Lee Kuan Yew, is remembered for his role in guiding a resource-scarce island nation to become water-self-sufficient despite many adversities.

PUB noted in a tribute statement that Lee Kuan Yew has left a great legacy. 'He was a visionary leader who designed Singapore's water story.'

Singapore's water story is a classic example of how a problem or adversity can lead to a revolutionary idea for the invention of Newater and making Singapore the world's top water technology nation.

Anyone who has conquered adversity will be someone who has done something valuable.

—Nelson Cheng

Do something great try conquering your problem.

—Nelson Cheng

What must I do to conquer my adversity?

CHAPTER 29

Turning Problems into Opportunities

Singapore's Case Study 02

What did Singapore do to overcome its national defence threats?

Suddenly, we're on our own. We have to defend ourselves. You have to build an army, navy, air force, control and command systems, early warning in the sky and so on.

—Lee Kuan Yew

Background of the Problem

In 1965, when Singapore was abruptly expelled from Malaysia, the odds were heavily stacked against its survival as a new sovereign state. Due to its small size, low population, lack of natural resources, and unpreparedness to defend itself, the island state was not likely to succeed on its own. As the newly independent nation had just separated from Malaysia, security was a major concern.

Due to Indonesia's armed campaign of *Konfrontasi*, Singapore was threatened with attacks.

'Suddenly, we're on our own. We have to defend ourselves You have to build an army, navy, air force, control and command systems, early warning in the sky, and so on,' he spoke with the *International Herald Tribune* in 2007 about that event.

Problem Exacerbated

Singapore was stunned when Britain announced that its troops would be withdrawn four years sooner than expected in 1968. The first batch of Singapore's 900 national servicemen were still training, and Singapore was not ready to defend itself.

The strong ties Mr Lee had with members of the British government helped to delay the withdrawal of British troops until late 1971, giving Singapore nine months to beef up its defences.

As a result of the withdrawal of British forces, the problem was further exacerbated. There was an urgent need to reinforce a fragile defence that had only two infantry battalions considering the impending withdrawal of British forces by 1975 (which was later changed to 1971).

Providing the Solution

During his tenure as minister for the Interior and Defence, the late Dr Goh Keng Swee was tasked with building up the Singapore Armed Forces (SAF). Lee personally sought foreign assistance as prime minister at the time to jumpstart the process.

The National Service, the Solution to the Problem

'I wanted the defence plan to aim at mobilising as large a part of the population as possible, in order to galvanise the people in their own defence while they had this strong feeling of patriotism as a result of their recent experiences,' Mr Lee wrote in his memoir *From Third World to First.*

So in 1967, he introduced National Service (NS), knowing that a large regular army would strain Singapore's limited manpower and financial resources. The Singapore Armed Forces (SAF) also benefited from Mr Lee's friendships with other world leaders throughout the years, securing training areas in Brunei, Thailand, Australia, and New Zealand.

Building a Talented World-Class Armed Force

As a means of attracting the best talents to the SAF, Mr Lee proposed the SAF Overseas Scholarship scheme in 1971, which Dr Goh refined. He explained in his memoirs: 'Without a yearly intake of about 10 of our best students, the SAF would have the military hardware but without the brainpower to use them to best advantage.'

Students with the best academic records were attracted to the scheme over the years. Four SAF scholars who rose to senior positions and later entered politics were mentioned by Mr Lee: the current prime minister Lee Hsieh Loong, Deputy Prime Minister Teo Chee Hean, former minister for Trade and Industry Lim Hng Kiang, and former minister for Foreign Affairs George Yeo.

'From the day we started, I knew that we needed a strong SAF, and I believe that still remains today. Without a strong SAF, there is no economic future, there is no security,' Mr Lee Kuan Yew told SAF officers at the Temasek Society's thirtieth-anniversary dinner dialogue in 2012.

The new generation of Singaporeans can learn from Mr Lee's experiences thanks to the books he wrote in his twilight years. 'My abiding concern for Singapore arises from my belief that the younger generation, especially those below 35, had never seen the harsh economic conditions. They, therefore, do not know the threats we face from neighbouring countries,' he wrote in *Hard Truths to Keep Singapore Going.*

On 23 Mar, he passed away at the age of ninety-one.

We are thankful for his contributions to the nation. He will be remembered for generations.

If you, who are growing up, do not understand that you have to defend this, then, in the end, we will lose. Other people will come, smack you down, and take over.
—Mr Lee, in discussing the importance of NS in 1967

The Golden Jubilee celebration of Singapore was spectacular in 2015. Despite the odds against its survival, the once fledging state prospered economically in the process.

A key component of the Singapore economic miracle is the physical security provided by the Singapore Armed Forces (SAF), which have been in place since independence and built upon military conscription first introduced—albeit amid controversy and opposition—when Singapore was still a British colony in 1954.

Having been re-instituted in 1967, this time on a bigger scale and with a post-independence populace unaccustomed to soldiering, National Service (NS) has grown a lot since then.

Singapore's National Service not only forms the backbone of the country's defence, but it has also become part of the nation's psyche and a non-negotiable requirement of citizenship, which is a way of life and a rite of passage for its male citizens, who bear disproportionately the burden and responsibilities of national defence.

An overview of the history and administration of the National Service in Singapore between 1954 and 2017. The article discusses not only the rationale for National Service and its underpinning principles but also how the city-state faced the burdens and challenges of imposing common defence responsibilities on its male citizens.

Conscription in Singapore reveals how the continuous engagement of its citizens is necessary to win the hearts and minds of each generation of Singaporeans and get them to embrace the concept of lifelong national service.

Without the defence capability that National Service made possible, Singapore may not have survived—let alone prospered . . . More than anything else, it is the spirit and commitment of our National Servicemen that makes the Singapore Armed Forces a potent and credible fighting force.
—Extract of speech by Prime Minister Lee Hsien Loon,
the eldest son of Lee Kuan Yew at the 40 Years of
National Service Commemoration Dinner
at Pasir Laba Camp

The SAF is today the most advanced armed forces in Asia, and indeed a potent credible fighting force with the capacity to deter all foreign threats.

This classic example shows how if we are resilient enough to solve a problem, a problem can become an opportunity.

How can I turn an existential problem into ab opportunity by solving it?

CHAPTER 30

Turning Problems into Opportunities Author's Case Study 01

The invention of a solution to a problem.

If we're not all enthusiastic about history, we still might benefit from learning about other people's past experiences.

—Nelson Cheng

It is the ability of everyone regardless of their circumstances to provide solutions or create inventions to their problems.

—Nelson Cheng

As mentioned in the preface of this book, the author's life-proven experience and innovative solutions to turning problems into opportunities are herewith illustrated over the next few chapters of his case studies.

He also explains what motivated him, as well as how some of the problems he encountered turned into ground-breaking inventions that turned into profitable business opportunities.

Readers will learn about the background leading to the invention while solving a problem, ascertaining the cause of the problem, and providing the solution, the genesis of the invention, and the detailed information of the author's invention,

When compared to the preceding chapters that contain concise information, the following case histories provide more detailed details about his inventions

Why Is the Author Writing a Case Study?

In the case study, the author discusses a method of research that he often used to solve problems in his business, etc. The method does not have a particular definition. An intensive, interdisciplinary study of multiple subjects makes up this case study. He aims to broaden the scope of its application to solving problems.

As part of his case study, the author examines in-depth data relating to several variables while attempting to provide a solution through an invention. He conducts an intensive, systematic analysis of a particular situation or problem faced by a person.

What Is the Purpose of the Case Study?

He describes a particular situation/problem he faced and how he turned the problem-solving situation into an opportunity via his invention.

Through his case studies, readers can gain insight into other people's perspectives on real-life business challenges or decision-making processes in a logical, professional, and ethical manner.

The aim of his case study is to describe an individual situation (case) or a problem encountered by the author, how he identifies the key issues associated with the case or problem, analysis of the case or a problem using relevant theoretical concepts from his unit or discipline; and ultimately suggest a course of action or solution for the case or problem.

By providing case studies, the author is attempting to provide insight into when this approach should be used, as well as a summary of key methodological considerations in relation to his method for solving problems, by first determining the cause of the problem and then finding a solution by modifying his inventions.

The problems of yesterday help you prepare for the challenges of today and the opportunities of tomorrow.

—Nelson Cheng

What are the key elements of a case history?

CHAPTER 31

Turning Problems into Opportunities
Author's Case History 02
Due to the high probability of hospital personnel contaminating surgical masks and gowns with Covid-19, disinfectants for surgical masks were developed.

Citizen mobilisation is needed once again to fight this Covid-19 pandemic. The fight against this deadly pandemic requires creative solutions and the use of all available means.

—Nelson Cheng

The human mind is capable of discovering solutions to problems or creating inventions irrespective of one's current circumstances.

—Nelson Cheng

As mentioned in the preface of this book the author's life-proven experience and innovative solutions to turning problems into opportunities are herewith illustrated over the next few chapters of his case studies.

Readers will learn about the background, genesis, and detailed information of the author's invention, rationale, and process, as well as how some of the problems he encountered were turned into ground-breaking inventions that turned into profitable business opportunities.

Comparatively to all the preceding chapters which are concise, the following case histories contain more information of his inventions. The following case histories demonstrate how the author turned obstacles into opportunities.

People's problem-solving styles are reflective of their unique personal characteristics in terms of how they respond to problem and how they position themselves in relation to a problem within the world.

—Nelson Cheng

Background Leading to the Invention

During an epidemic or pandemic, disposable surgical face masks and sleeved gowns are the most used items by healthcare professionals and the public. It helps to catch the bacteria shed in liquid droplets during sneezing into the mouth and nose of caregivers when wearing a disposable surgical mask or sleeved gown made from hydrophilic or hydrophobic materials.

When there is an epidemic or a pandemic outbreak, surgical face masks and gowns are ubiquitous. It has long been believed that face masks protect patients against wound infection and contamination by surgeons and other healthcare providers. As a protective barrier, it protects the user from a variety of hazards, such as splashes of large droplets of body fluids. As well as protecting the wearer from infection, surgical masks also protect other people from infection.

During the outbreak of the Covid-19 in January 2020, a global shortage of disposable facial masks and gowns resulted in the disease spreading at an unprecedented rate throughout the world. Since China, the factory of the world, was affected by the virus, there was a global shortage of disposable facial masks and gowns. In response to this need, the author and his team develop top-of-the-line facial masks and surgical gown disinfectants.

The chance of a hospital staff member contaminating surgical masks and gowns with Covid-19 and other bacteria is extremely high. Both healthcare professionals and patients can benefit from wearing disposable clothing and personal protective equipment that is antimicrobial coated.

Everyone, including healthcare professionals, should avoid inhaling airborne bacteria or virus particles during an epidemic or pandemic situation. The presence of viruses and bacteria on surgical masks, sleeves, and other protective gear can have dire consequences for the wearers of those gears. For the protection of healthcare professionals and users of said gears, the author saw a critical need to develop a disinfectant that features silver nanoparticles impregnating these gears with good residual effects that will inactivate any enveloped viruses and bacteria on masks and gowns.

The Genesis of the Invention

The invention here has been developed to address the problem of inactivating bacteria and enveloped viruses such as coronavirus, SARS, MERS, influenza A, and influenza B on disposable surgical masks and sleeved gowns worn by healthcare professionals and the public at large during an outbreak or epidemic.

Nonwoven fabric is used to make these surgical face masks, which are better at filtering bacteria and allowing airflow than a woven cloth.

Polypropylene is the material most used to make masks, a type of fabric made from a thermoplastic polymer. Surgical masks are also available in blue in polystyrene, polycarbonate, polyethylene, or polyester, which all derive their materials from thermoplastic polymers.

As surgical masks and gowns are hydrophobic, they require a suitable disinfectant for the impregnation process, and there was a global shortage of both masks and gowns in early 2020.

Determine the Problems and Provide Solutions

In light of knowledge about the materials used in protective gear, the author and his team developed a specially formulated impregnating solution for masks and gowns. That solution displays a disinfecting efficacy of 99.999 per cent with excellent residual efficacy of up to eight hours properties.

Henceforth, a potent chemical composition containing aqueous colloidal silver nanoparticles, isopropanol/ethanol alcohol, chlorhexidine gluconate, peppermint/spearmint essential oils with colloidal silver nanoparticles was developed.

A Detailed Description of the Invention

The invention consists of aqueous colloidal silver nanoparticles with a size range of 2–150 nm that are used to increase the residual efficacy of a disinfectant impregnated into disposable surgical masks and gowns.

Silver nanoparticles are extremely small, resulting in the particles having a large surface area compared to their volume.

As a result, they can easily interact with other particles and become more effective antibacterial agents. The effect can be so great that one gram of silver nanoparticles can give antibacterial properties to hundreds of square metres of the substrate material.

This makes disposable surgical gowns and sleeved gowns commercially viable for impregnation. There have been numerous applications of silver's antimicrobial effect against different types of microorganisms.

Silver bactericidal properties come from its ability to bind to the disulfide or sulfhydryl groups in bacterial cell walls. Nanoparticles of silver also bind DNA.

During these binding events, metabolic processes are disrupted, resulting in the death of cells.

The isopropanol/ethanol alcohol is added to the chemical composition to kill bacteria by destroying their peptidoglycan/lipopolysaccharide cell walls and inactivate enveloped viruses by denaturing the capsid protein. In addition, it enhances the hydrophilic properties of peppermint/spearmint essential oils used in the chemical formulation

In another embodiment, chlorhexidine gluconate/quaternary ammonium compounds (alkyl dimethyl benzyl ammonium chloride, alkyl didecyl dimethyl ammonium chloride, and dialkyl dimethyl ammonium chloride) are employed to kill bacteria, fungi, viruses, and protozoa.

Its ability to neutralise Gram-positive bacteria, Gram-negative bacteria, and fungi make chlorhexidine the preferred choice due to its broad-spectrum biocide property. It has both bacteriostatic and bactericidal properties, making it an excellent choice for an impregnation composition for surgical masks and sleeved surgical gowns.

The peppermint/spearmint essential oils are added to the chemical composition to enhance its antimicrobial properties. The antimicrobial properties of peppermint essential oil make it the preferred essential oil to use against both Gram-positive and Gram-negative bacteria. The essential oil of peppermint has antiviral and fungicidal properties as well.

Water plays an important role in denaturing the capsid proteins of enveloping viruses and bacterial cell membranes. In addition, it acts as a carrier for all the ingredients of the said chemical composition.

The inevitable problem of healthcare staff contaminating surgical masks and gowns with Covid-19, prompted the author to develop the highly effective Legionella-X mask disinfectant.

Don't wait for opportunities to come your way, take advantage of common occurrences of problems, and turn them into opportunities.

—Nelson Cheng

Is there a current problem I can solve in this pandemic?

CHAPTER 32

Turning Problems into Opportunities Author's Case History 03

The problems associated with infections caused by surfaces contaminated with Covid-19 led to the invention of a self-disinfecting coating of the author.

Citizen mobilisation is needed once again to fight this Covid-19 pandemic. The fight against this deadly pandemic requires creative solutions and the use of all available means.

—Nelson Cheng

Use problems as opportunities instead of waiting for them to present themselves.

—Nelson Cheng

As mentioned in the preface of this book, the author's life-proven experience and innovative solutions to turning problems into opportunities are herewith illustrated over the next few chapters of his case studies.

Readers will learn about the background, genesis, and detailed information of the author's invention, rationale, and process, as well as how some of the problems he encountered were turned into ground-breaking inventions that turned into profitable business opportunities.

The Invention of Legionella-X Viral Shield, a Self-Disinfecting Coating for Hard Surfaces.

Background Leading to the Invention

Coronaviruses can persist on surfaces like countertops and doorknobs for several hours to days at a time. The time they survive depends on the material they are made of. Covid-19 belongs to the same family as viruses that can live on surfaces we come in contact every day.

Therefore, to prevent any infections from touching the contaminated surfaces, it is imperative to disinfect all surfaces as frequently as possible in public places and on board mass rapid trains, buses, taxis, etc. On the other hand, where human traffic is extremely heavy, this may not be feasible or even convenient.

The author realised there was a need to develop a self-disinfecting coating that could inactivate bacteria, viruses, and fungi, because the disinfecting efficacy of current common disinfectants against viruses, bacteria, and microorganisms such as fungi depends on several factors, some of which are inherent in the organism and some of which stem from the external environment, including chemical and physical factors.

The Genesis of the Invention

Microorganisms differ in their intrinsic resistance mechanisms to disinfectants. Spores, for instance, have a coating and cortex that help them to resist disinfectants, mycobacteria have a waxy cell wall that helps to prevent disinfectants from getting in, and Gram-negative bacteria possess an outer membrane that helps to prevent disinfectants from entering. To make the self-disinfecting coating effective, a dual inactivation mechanism is necessary. A biofilm consists of a group of microorganisms that can grow on a wide variety of surfaces. There are many types of microorganisms that form biofilms, including bacteria, fungi, and protists.

Biofilms or thick masses of extracellular material protect microorganisms from most disinfectants. It is a microbial community that is tightly attached to a surface and cannot be easily removed. Microbes within these masses can become resistant to disinfectants by a variety of mechanisms, including their physical characteristics, their genotypes, their production of neutralising enzymes, and their physiologic gradients within the biofilm (e.g., pH). In biofilms, bacteria are up to 1,000 times more resistant to antimicrobials than they are in suspension.

Determine the Problems and Provide Solutions

Aside from the inefficiency of the common disinfectants, several physical and chemical factors also influence disinfectant procedures: temperature, pH, relative humidity, and water hardness.

A common practice is to raise the temperature in order to increase the effectiveness of disinfectants. The temperature increase can also degrade the disinfectant and weaken its germicidal properties, which may pose a health hazard.

Since current disinfectants have the above deficiencies, there is an urgent need for a revolutionary self-disinfecting coating that utilises reactive oxygen species (ROS) and denaturation to destroy viruses, bacteria, and fungi, since common disinfectants cannot solve all the above problems.

A detailed Description of the Invention

The author discovered that a self-disinfecting coating can be highly effective against viruses, bacteria, and fungi when using dual inactivation mechanisms. An innovative self-disinfecting coating system with dual inactivation mechanisms can inactivate viruses, bacteria, and fungi with 99.99 per cent efficiency using colloidal silver nanoparticles, colloidal copper nanoparticles, quaternary ammonium compound, chlorhexidine, and silicone emulsion.

Using reactive oxygen species (ROS) derived from a solution containing colloidal silver nanoparticles and copper nanoparticles in combination with denaturation inactivation mechanisms using quaternary ammonium compounds, this invention is directed to use dual inactivation mechanisms method against viruses, bacteria, and fungi of the self-disinfecting coating.

Another embodiment of the self-disinfecting coating uses chlorhexidine as the denaturation mechanism against both Gram-positive and Gram-negative bacteria.

The self-disinfecting coating of the duality inactivation mechanism is also fabricated with silicone emulsion as a clear residual film. For the formulation of synergistic chemicals, water is used as a carrier.

In figure 1, the reactive oxygen species are used in the dual inactivation mechanisms of the self-disinfecting coating to inactivate colloidal silver nanoparticles and copper nanoparticles.

Here, we describe how silver and copper nanoparticles inactivate.

To kill microbes, silver nanoparticles continuously release silver ions. Silver and copper ions adhere to cell walls and cytoplasmic membranes due to their electrostatic attraction and affinity for sulphur proteins.

By adhering to the cytoplasmic membrane, the ions can increase permeability and lead to disruption of the bacterial envelope. In the presence of free silver and copper ions, respiratory enzymes can be deactivated, resulting in reactive oxygen species but preventing adenosine triphosphate production.

The production of reactive oxygen species is the principal mechanism for the disruption of cell membranes and modification of DNA.

A description of the inactivation mechanism via denaturation of the quaternary ammonium compound of the self-disinfecting coating follows figure 2.

Upon contact with the bacteria cell wall, quaternary ammonium compound will disrupt the lipid membrane, thinning the bacteria cell wall. The thinning process will result in the leakage of cytosolic contents. In addition, precipitation of cellular material will be facilitated. Destroying essential gradients will ultimately lead to destruction.

Following is a description of the inactivation mechanism via denaturation of the self-disinfecting coating in figure 3.

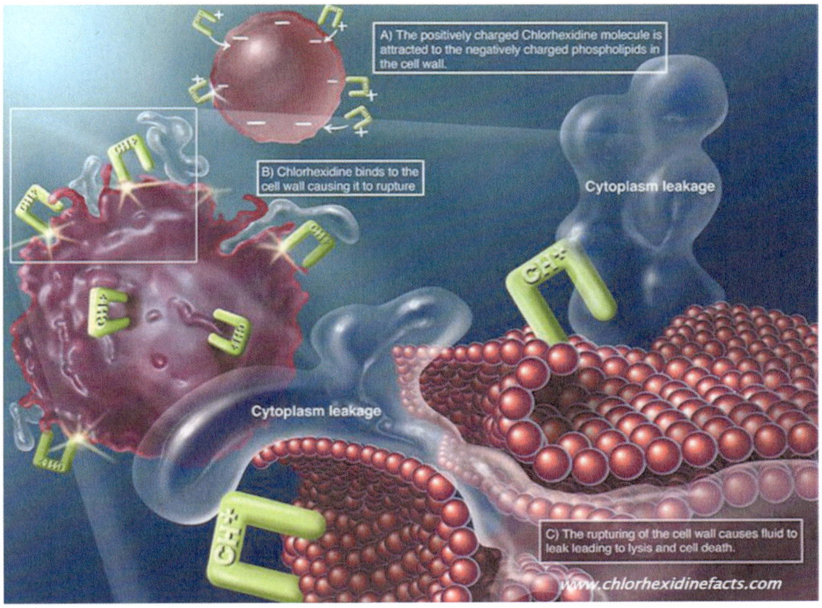

Figure 3

The negatively charged phospholipids in the cell wall are attracted to the positively charged chlorhexidine molecule. Chlorhexidine causes the cell wall to rupture, causing cytoplasm leakage. When the cell wall ruptures, the fluid leaks, resulting in lysis and cell death.

The problems associated with infections caused by contaminated surfaces with Covid-19 led to the invention of a self-disinfecting coating of the author.

How has this chapter influenced me?

CHAPTER 33

Turning Problems into Opportunities Author's Case History 04

The problem of poor indoor air quality is one of the contributing factors to the spread of infectious diseases that led to the development of self-disinfecting coating.

Citizen mobilisation is needed once again to fight this Covid-19 pandemic. The fight against this deadly pandemic requires creative solutions and the use of all available means.

—Nelson Cheng

Several infectious diseases have been shown to spread through HVAC systems, including measles, tuberculosis, chickenpox, influenza, smallpox, H1N1 influenza epidemic in 2011, and the Middle East respiratory syndrome (MERS) and SARS.

As mentioned in the preface of this book, the author's life-proven experience and innovative solutions to turning problems into opportunities are herewith illustrated over the next few chapters of his case studies.

Readers will learn about the background, genesis, and detailed information of the author's invention, rationale, and process, as well as how some of the problems he encountered were turned into ground-breaking inventions that turned into profitable business opportunities.

The Invention of a Self-Disinfecting Coating on Air-Conditioner Filters

Background Leading to the Invention

In humid climates, air conditioners are a necessity. Air conditioners remove hot, humid air from enclosed spaces and replace it with cooler air. An air conditioner poses the biggest threat to indoor air quality due to the presence of microorganisms.

In the current Covid-19 epidemic, indoor air pollutants are being cited as a public health issue and an important factor to be considered for controlling the spread of diseases in an enclosed environment.

Research shows that some microorganisms can colonise filters in air conditioners. Microorganisms have been observed to grow and reproduce more rapidly when incubated for longer periods. Microorganisms, namely fungi, have been shown to colonise air-conditioning filter materials

Indoor air can contain fungi, pathogenic bacteria, and viruses, resulting in allergic and infectious illnesses, respiratory ailments, and hypersensitivity reactions. The symptoms of this group include throat irritation, eye irritation, nose irritation, sinus congestion, headaches, etc.

The Genesis of the Invention

Most airborne infectious diseases are transmitted indoors, where 90 per cent of people spend most of their time. A person infected with coronavirus spreads it through airborne droplets when coughing or sneezing. Coronavirus particles can survive on surfaces for some time, but the extent to which they do so is dependent on factors like temperature and humidity.

In early studies, researchers found that the survival of a virus was dependent upon the type of surface it landed on. Coronaviruses can live between three hours and seven days, depending on the material. When an infected person breathes, sneezes, or coughs out infectious particles, the air conditioner system will draw in those particles and blow them back into the room, putting everyone in the room at risk.

In poor indoor air, bacteria, fungi, and viruses contribute to the spread of infectious diseases and a variety of respiratory disorders.

Determine the Problems and Provide Solutions

Research studies have established that several infectious diseases have been shown to spread through HVAC systems, including measles, tuberculosis, chickenpox, influenza, smallpox, H1N1 influenza epidemic in 2011, and the Middle East respiratory syndrome (MERS) and SARS.

Some microorganisms only require a certain amount of water in the air to reproduce and grow. It is very likely that air-conditioning systems are a route for the transmission of bacteria and fungi found on air conditioner filters, especially in tropical regions.

People with immune compromise, as well as those with cancer, transplant patients, and HIV/AIDS patients, can be at risk from the presence of bacteria such as Bacillus, Providencia, Clostridium, Acinetobacter, Aspergillus, and Cladosporium.

The transmission rate would be reduced if the number of infectious particles indoors was reduced. When an infected person exhales those infectious particles, the air conditioner will collect those particles and return them to the room.

After considering the above, the author felt that air-conditioning filters should be disinfected as often as possible to ensure that indoor spaces are safe and that air circulating in enclosed spaces is free of pathogens.

To combat the proliferation of microorganisms and viruses and the hassle of disinfecting air-con filters, a self-disinfecting coating has been invented to prevent the breeding of microorganisms and viruses.

A Detailed Description of the Invention

A synergistic solution of quaternary ammonium compounds, colloidal silver, copper nanoparticles, and others makes up the self-disinfecting coating. The inactivation of viruses and killing of the microorganism is achieved through both denaturation and reactive oxygen species.

The synergistic process using reactive oxygen species (ROS) from silver nanoparticles and denaturation by quaternary ammonium compound (QAC) and chlorhexidine is described below.

Silver nanoparticles in the self-disinfecting coating will facilitate the production of reactive oxygen species (ROS), an unstable molecule containing oxygen that reacts readily with other molecules in the cell. Any accumulation of ROS in the cell may damage DNA, RNA, and proteins, resulting in cell death.

Therefore, ROS are free oxygen radicals. Through the self-disinfecting mechanism, bacteria and microorganisms encountering the filters will be obliterated.

The silver nanoparticle self-disinfecting coating will release silver ions (Ag+), which will disrupt bacteria's cell walls and cytoplasmic membranes as they adhere to or pass through them.

Protein synthesis is then inhibited after the denaturation of ribosomes occurs. The production of adenosine triphosphate (ATP) will be interrupted because silver ions deactivate respiratory enzymes in the cytoplasm, resulting in the production of reactive oxygen species (ROS). Disruption of membranes occurs when reactive oxygen species are generated.

Silver and reactive oxygen species bind to deoxyribonucleic acid, preventing its replication and multiplication. Denaturation of the membrane occurs when silver nanoparticles accumulate in cell wall pits. Denaturation of the membrane allows silver nanoparticles to cross directly across the cytoplasmic membrane, allowing organelles to be released from cells.

By the loss of osmotic balance, proteins, enzymes, coenzymes, ribonucleic acids, and metabolites leak into the cell, resulting in the inability of adenosine triphosphate to be reconstituted.

Below are drawings illustrating the obliteration mechanisms of the self-disinfecting coating.

As shown in drawings 1 and 2, the silver ions (Ag+) released by silver nanoparticles in the self-disinfecting coating can adhere to or pass through the bacterial cell wall and cytoplasmic membrane.

In drawing 3, it can be seen that once the cell wall and the cytoplasmic membrane are ruptured, the denaturation of ribosomes will occur, inhibiting protein synthesis.

The production of adenosine triphosphate (ATP) will be disrupted by silver ions, which deactivate respiratory enzymes on the cytoplasmic membrane, as shown in drawing 4.

The reactive oxygen species (ROS) are then produced. As illustrated in drawing 5, reactive oxygen species cause membrane disruption.

After binding to the deoxyribonucleic acid, the silver nanoparticles and reactive oxygen species will block its replication and prevent cell proliferation, as illustrated in drawing 6.

In drawing 7, silver nanoparticles have accumulated in the pits of the cell wall, causing denaturation of the membrane.

Denaturation of the membrane allows silver nanoparticles to cross directly across the cytoplasmic membrane, allowing organelles to be released from cells

Drawing 8 illustrates in detail the mechanism of inactivating the reactive oxygen species of silver and nanoparticles against the cells of microorganisms.

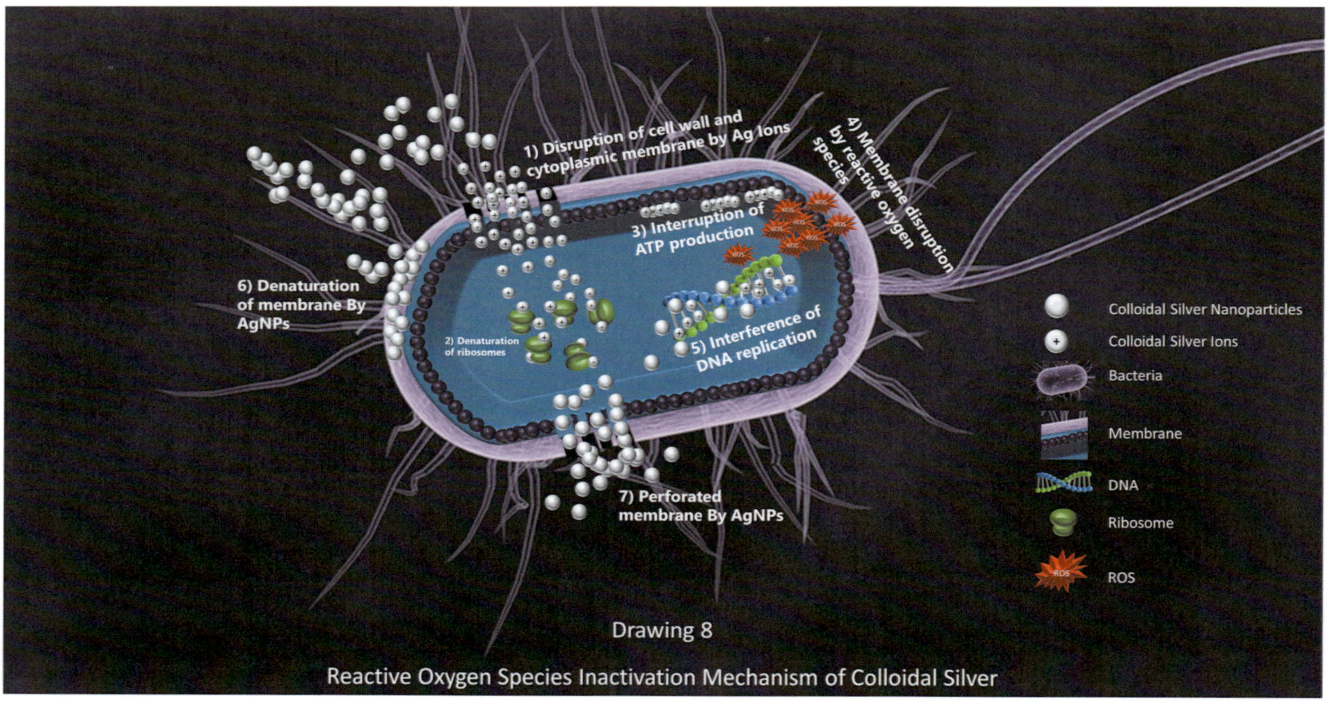

Drawing 8

Reactive Oxygen Species Inactivation Mechanism of Colloidal Silver

Quaternary ammonium compounds inactivate energy-producing enzymes in the self-disinfecting coating. Cell membranes are disrupted, and essential proteins are denaturised. These are positively charged cationic surfactants (surface-active agents) that have a profound effect on cell walls and membranes after prolonged contact. These molecules have a permanent positive charge that enables them to bind readily to microbes that have a negative charge. The stability of QACs is unaffected by pH. It remains effective even when prolonged contact with inanimate surfaces occurs. A quaternary ammonium compound inactivates the cell of the microorganism as illustrated in figures 9 and 10.

Drawing 9 shows the membrane of bacteria, and drawing 10 shows the introduction of the quaternary ammonium compound from the self-disinfecting coating. A positively charged surfactant like QAC readily binds to negatively charged membranes.

In drawing 12, the QAC adheres to the membrane due to the different polarities, resulting in the thinning and disruption of the membrane.

The rupture or disruption of the membrane results in the leakage of cytosolic contents, the precipitation of cellular materials, and their entrapment in the QAC, as shown in drawings 13 and 14.

Chlorhexidine serves as a co-denaturing agent in the self-disinfecting coating.

The self-disinfecting coating contains chlorhexidine, a cationic bisbiguanide that can kill Gram-positive and Gram-negative bacteria and fungi. Bacteriostatic (inhibits bacterial growth) and bactericidal (kills bacteria) actions are among its mechanisms.

Positively charged chlorhexidine binds to negatively charged phospholipids in the cell wall. It damages a cell's wall through osmosis. The cationic molecule produces a bactericidal effect when it binds to the bacterial cell wall. Chlorohexidine inactivates microorganisms through a mechanism illustrated in drawing 15.

An extended period makes chlorhexidine effective against a broad spectrum of bacteria and fungi. Chlorhexidine is slowly released and kills microorganisms by disrupting their membranes because of its substantivity. These properties are not found in quaternary ammonium compounds. In drawing 16, it causes cell death because it leaks components. Chlorhexidine congeals or solidifies the cytoplasm at high concentrations.

Chlorhexidine begins working as soon as it is absorbed by bacteria. Even in low doses, it affects the integrity of the cell wall. Chlorhexidine enters the cytoplasmic membrane (inner membrane) of a broken cell and attacks it. Damage to the semipermeable membrane of the cytoplasm, as shown in drawing 17, will cause the cell to die.

Silicone emulsion fluid from the self-disinfecting coating is used for the residual film-forming coating. It was used in the self-disinfecting coating because of its non-toxic properties, inert properties, heat stability, glossy appearance, and antistatic nature. Silicone emulsion can be used for either the non-ionic or ionic self-disinfecting coating because it is non-ionic.

The problems associated with infections caused by air-con filters contaminated with Covid-19 led to the invention of a self-disinfecting coating of the author.

Having faced adversity, what did I learn?

CHAPTER 34

Turning Problems into Opportunities Author's Case History 05

The problem of infection entering through the nose prompted the development of antimicrobial nasal sprays to prevent upper respiratory tract infections.

Citizen mobilisation is needed once again to fight this Covid-19 pandemic. The fight against this deadly pandemic requires creative solutions and the use of all available means.

—Nelson Cheng

Legionella-X Silver Nanoparticles Nasal Spray as a Prophylactic Therapy against Covid-19 Infection

As mentioned in the preface of this book, the author's life-proven experience and innovative solutions to turning problems into opportunities are herewith illustrated over the next few chapters of his case studies.

Readers will learn about the background, genesis, and detailed information of the author's invention, rationale, and process, as well as how some of the problems he encountered were turned into ground-breaking inventions that turned into profitable business opportunities.

The Background Leading the Invention

Globally, more than 2.5 million people have died because of the Covid-19 pandemic as of 23 February 2021. Nanoparticles of colloidal silver exhibit antimicrobial properties. Nanoparticles of colloidal silver have been extensively used in wound care.

Infectious agents such as viruses and bacteria enter the body through the nose, which is both a source of pathogens and an entry point for them. According to accepted pathogenesis models, Covid-19 respiratory infections are generally entered mildly in the nasal cavity or upper respiratory tract.

The upper respiratory system, which includes the nose, mouth, and throat, is most affected by an initial viral infection such as Covid-19, before moving on to the lower respiratory system, which includes the diaphragm and lungs as shown in picture A.

The Genesis of the Invention

A novel therapy that targets respiratory infections at an early stage, i.e., when they affect primarily the upper respiratory system and bronchial tree, have great potential for treating respiratory infections.

In a confirmed case of Covid-19, the virus is detected via nasopharyngeal and oropharyngeal swabs. Due to the cell receptor angiotensin converting enzyme 2 for Covid-19, studies have shown the oral cavity to be a potential route for infection with Covid-19. It is therefore important to sanitise the upper respiratory tract during the early stages of infection or as a preventive measure by using sanitising nasal sprays.

Determine the Problem and Provide the Solution

When a person coughs, sneezes, or talks, a mixture of saliva and fluids are released from the mouth and nose. Based on the particle size and environmental conditions, the said mixture droplets may contribute to viral transmission to anyone nearby.

Mouth and nose are important reservoirs of oral opportunistic pathogens and infectious viruses. To reduce the severity of the infection and to reduce transmission, it is crucial to reduce the viral load in the oral cavity by using a nasal spray while the infection is still at its earliest stages.

By arresting the potential issue before it becomes problematic, prophylaxis prevents unintended problems. Disease prevention is often easier, less expensive, and less painful than treating it after it deteriorates. Providing it before or after a patient has been exposed to an infectious agent, but before serious symptoms have appeared, will help that patient's immune system combat a serious infection.

Prophylactic therapy refers to preventative treatment that takes many forms and continues even after a disease process is diagnosed. The term *prophylaxis* is not limited to preventing disease, but may also include preventing a worsening of disease, minimising the severity of the disease and preventing overtreatment through the early detection and treatment of infection.

For this reason, Legionella-X Nasal Spray was developed specifically for use with prophylactic antimicrobial agents for upper respiratory tract infections.

Detailed Description of the Invention

Formulation of the nasal spray. Colloidal silver nanoparticles solutions were designed based on the interaction mechanism of the SARS-CoV-2 virus with the membrane of the nasal tissue. The virus depends on its spike protein to entry in the host cell and survive. In this sense, formulation must include a supporting molecule capable to capped AgNPs and provide a chemical functional group able to serve as an interface between the virus and the nasal tissue cells.

To improve the efficiency of the nasal spray regarding to the maximum surface covering and wetting, an ethoxylated sorbitan mono oleate surfactant (Tween 80) was added. Chlorhexidine digluconate was then added to the silver nanoparticles solution to enhance its bactericidal properties.

Chlorhexidine digluconate exhibits good bactericidal and virucidal activity against enveloped viruses such as coronaviruses. The bactericidal activity is caused by the nonspecific binding of the positively charged chlorhexidine molecule to the membrane phospholipids of bacteria.

The chlorhexidine molecule has positive charges at each end. Bacteria and yeast cells tend to have negatively charged areas on their exteriors, and their interaction with chlorhexidine causes damage to the cell membranes of the microbes. The bactericidal activity is caused by the binding of the positively charged chlorhexidine molecule to the membrane phospholipids of bacteria.

Based on the viral entry of infection, it was seen as an opportunity to develop an antimicrobial nasal spray to be used with prophylactic antimicrobial agents to prevent upper respiratory tract infections. Therefore, Legionella-X Silver Nanoparticles Nasal Spray was developed as a prophylactic therapy against Covid-19 infection with an efficacy of 99.9999 per cent against both positive and negative bacteria.

Test Report on the efficacy of Legionella-X Nasal Spray

TEST REPORT: 7191262105-CHM21-02-RC

Date: 23 JUN 2021 Tel: +65 69736171

Client's Ref: - Email: Randy.CHIN@tuvsud.com

Note: This report is issued subject to the Testing and Certification Regulations of the TÜV SÜD Group and the General Terms and Conditions of Business of TÜV SÜD PSB Pte Ltd. In addition, this report is governed by the terms set out within this report.

PSB Singapore

Add value. Inspire trust.

SUBJECT

Antibacterial Activity Evaluation

CLIENT

Magna International Pte Ltd
10H Enterprise Road
Singapore 629834

SAMPLE SUBMISSION DATE/ TEST DATE

31 May 2021 / 02 Jun 2021

DESCRIPTION OF SAMPLE

One sample was submitted, labelled as follows:

Product Description	:	Legionella-X Nasal Spray (Silver Nanoparticles Fortified with Chlorohexidine)
Batch no.	:	nil
Manufacturer	:	Magna International Pte Ltd

METHOD OF TEST

BS EN 1040 : 2005

"Chemical disinfectants and antiseptics – Quantitative suspension test for the evaluation of basic bactericidal activity of chemical disinfectants and antiseptics – Test method and requirements (Phase 1)".

The test microorganisms used were :

Pseudomonas aeruginosa (ATCC 15442)
Staphylococcus aureus (ATCC 6538)

Dilution tested : Neat
Contact time : 5 minutes
Neutralization method: DE Broth Neutralization
Test temperature: 20±1°C
Incubation temperature: 36±1°C

TÜV SÜD PSB

Laboratory:
TÜV SÜD PSB Pte. Ltd.
15 International Business Park
TÜV SÜD @ IBP
Singapore 609937

Phone : +65-6778 7777
E-mail: info.sg@tuvsud.com
https://www.tuvsud.com/sg
Co. Reg : 199002667R

Regional Head Office:
TÜV SÜD Asia Pacific Pte. Ltd.
15 International Business Park
TÜV SÜD @ IBP
Singapore 609937

Page 1 of 5

What can I do to thrive during a pandemic?

CHAPTER 35

Turning Problems into Opportunities Author's Case History 06

The problems of cleaning barrels of main battle tanks and howitzer artillery guns led to the invention of Vappro Automatic Cleaner.

Take advantage of problems instead of waiting for them to manifest themselves.

—Nelson Cheng

As mentioned in the preface of this book, the author's life-proven experience and innovative solutions to turning problems into opportunities are herewith illustrated over the next few chapters of his case studies.

Readers will learn about the background, genesis, and detailed information of the author's invention, rationale, and process, as well as how some of the problems he encountered were turned into ground-breaking inventions that turned into profitable business opportunities.

The Invention of the Vappro (ABC) Automatic Gun Barrel Cleaner

Background Leading to the Invention

The author had succeeded in securing a large military contract to preserve the main battle tanks from an East Asian country against corrosion. In the context of preservation, the barrels of main battle tanks (MBTs) needed to be cleaned.

There were several hundred main battle tanks that needed to be preserved, so cleaning the gun barrel was the most tedious and time-consuming task. Just like any other contract, there were charges imposed for any delays.

According to the time-motion study conducted on the first preserved tank, the author realised that his company would not be able to complete the preservation by the contract's deadline. To improve the speed of gun barrel cleaning, a new approach was required.

The Genesis of Invention

Until the author's invention, gun barrels could only be cleaned with an abrasive hard brush, gun cleaning liquid, and a long pole as shown in picture 1. This was a time-consuming and laborious process. The barrel surface will also wear out faster, shortening the lifespan of a firearm.

Cleaning the gun barrels of the main battle tank was a tedious process that required many man-hours. The gun barrels of the main battle tanks were cleaned by means of a set of five-piece metal cleaning rods, each measuring more than 2 m attached together with a wire or hard brush. The internal surface of the barrel was cleaned by said brush by means of mechanical contact of the brush in forwards and backward movement. Usually, four to six men are deployed to carry out such tasks and often experience injury due to overstrained muscles. The long length of the attached cleaning rods required considerable additional space at both ends, making it extremely difficult for cleaning the gun barrel of the main battle tank, shown in picture 1.

The barrel and chamber of the main battle tank gun will be filled with particles of carbon, copper, lead, steel, and plastic each time the gun was fired. Therefore, over time, these particles would accumulate inside the bore. Once fouling occurred, the accuracy of the gun will be reduced and increased the chance of the gun misfiring. As shown in picture 2, rust is another common problem that must be addressed.

Determine the Problems and Provide Solutions

When the author realised the flaws in armed forces cleaning methodology, he created a novel and yet simple method involving the use of a winch apparatus consisting of pulling cables, retractor cables, remote switches, battery cables, and connection assembly, crank handles, safety latch hooks, and universal adapters, as shown in figure 1.

A Detailed Description of the Author's Invention

The winch had a pulling cable whose length ranged from 0.5 m to 30 m, as shown in figure 1. There is a battery terminal assembly on the side of the winch, along with positive and negative battery cables that range from 0.5 to 25 m long. A safety latch hook is attached to the retractor cable, which has a length ranging from 0.5 m to 30 m. The bore brush can be used to clean barrels with a diameter of 75 mm to 240 mm.

The Cleaning Process of the Author's Invention

The winch apparatus is mounted on the universal adapter assembly with a pulling cable extended and attached with a safety latch hook. Both gun barrel adapters for the gun barrel with and without a muzzle brake were also displayed in figure 2.

In figure 3 of the author's invention, the winch's pulling cable is attached to one of the eyehooks of the bore brush via a safety latch hook, and the retractor cable is attached to the other eyehook via a safety latch hook.

According to the author's invention showed in figure 4, a gun barrel without the muzzle brake (not part of the invention) is mounted with a cleaning winch via the gun barrel adapter. The gun barrel adapter is mounted on the universal adapter assembly of the winch.

In figure 5, a gun barrel mounted with a muzzle brake (not part of the invention) is attached via the gun barrel adapter to the cleaning winch. The gun barrel adapter is mounted on the universal adapter assembly of the winch.

Figures 6a and 6b illustrate the steps for setting up the apparatus for the cleaning process in accordance with the invention. The winch is attached to the gun barrel via a gun barrel adapter (applicable to a gun barrel with or without a muzzle) that is mounted on the universal adapter assembly of the winch. The winch battery cable assembly and the terminals of the twelve-volt battery are connected by battery terminal cables. Next, the winch remote switch is connected. After unlatching the winch, the pulling cable is released, after which the retractor is pushed to the front of the barrel via the breech block. Using safety latch hooks, the pulling cable is connected to the retractor cable and pulled to the barrel's end. This allows the bore brush to be attached.

In the cleaning method according to the invention shown in figure 7, the bore brush is sprayed with a cleaning solution with a hand sprayer. The cleaning solution dissolves carbon, corrosion, combustion ammunition residue, grease, and oil residues from the barrel.

The bore brush is sprayed soaking wet with the cleaning solution before being pulled through the barrel as shown in figure 8. The bore brush is guided into the barrel via the breech block that indicates the beginning of the cleaning process.

The invention shown in figures 9 and 9a shows how to clean a gun barrel. To pull through the barrel, the winch is turned on and the bore brush is guided into the gun barrel via the breech block. As the winch coils up the pulling cable, the bore brush slowly moves to the front of the barrel. This allows the bore brush to be removed from the retractor cable and pulling cable. For the second pull-through, the bore brush is carried by hand to the breech block. Meanwhile, the pulling cable is attached to the retractor cable via the safety latch hook and is pulled manually to the barrel breech block for attachment of the bore brush for the second pull-through of the barrel.

What Is the Significance of This invention?

Comparing the barrels cleaned by the invention with barrels cleaned by the traditional long-handled metal brush, 75 per cent more barrels were cleaned per day by two men than by six men using the traditional method.

By using the invention, no overstretched muscles were injured as compared to using a traditional long-handled metal brush, where four men were injured.

An endoscope was used to inspect the barrels, and it was determined that the barrels cleaned by the invention were in a significantly better condition; that is, they showed less wear and were pristine clean without any traces of carbon or combustion residue, as shown in the pictures below the conditions of the barrel before and after cleaning by automatic barrel cleaning winch.

An endoscope was used to inspect the barrels, and it was found barrel 1 was not fit-for-firing (FFF) despite being cleaned by a five-piece cleaning rod. As shown in picture barrel 1, rust stains and other deposits were clearly visible.

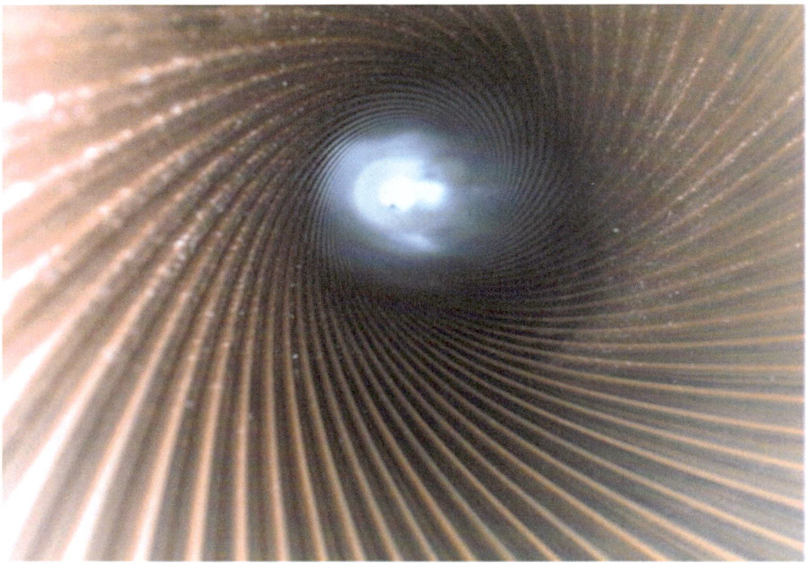

Barrel 1

In contrast, barrel 2 cleaned by the automatic barrel cleaner was in pristine condition.

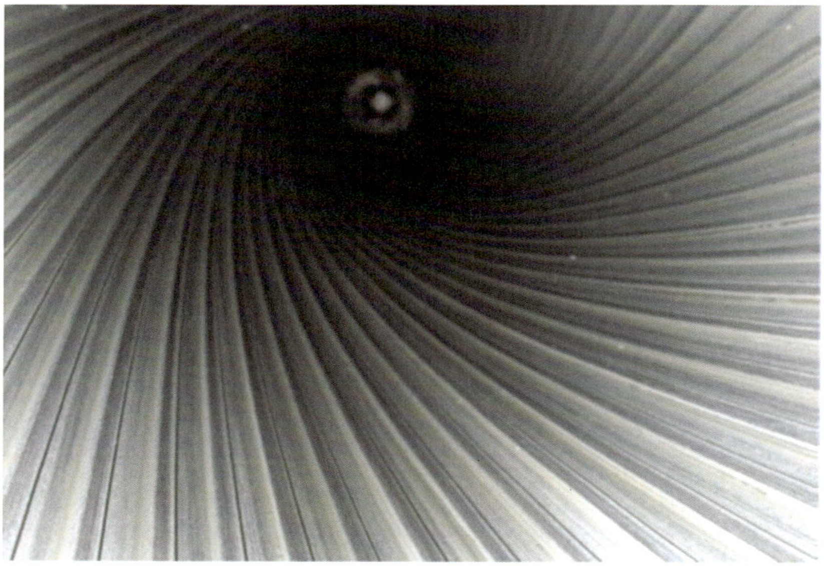

Barrel 2

Developed by the author to solve the tedious problem of cleaning gun barrels, Vappro Automatic Barrel Cleaner is being sold to armed forces all over the world.

In response to the global patent filing, he affirmed his conviction that we exist to solve problems for the benefit of society.

Publication of Vappro ABC in WIPO

(12) INTERNATIONAL APPLICATION PUBLISHED UNDER THE PATENT COOPERATION TREATY (PCT)

(19) **World Intellectual Property Organization**
International Bureau

PCT

(43) **International Publication Date**
9 July 2009 (09.07.2009)

(10) **International Publication Number**
WO 2009/085013 A1

(51) **International Patent Classification:**
F41A 29/00 (2006.01) *F41A 29/02* (2006.01)

(21) **International Application Number:** PCT/SG2008/000016

(22) **International Filing Date:** 15 January 2008 (15.01.2008)

(25) **Filing Language:** English

(26) **Publication Language:** English

(30) **Priority Data:**
200719154-7 31 December 2007 (31.12.2007) SG

(71) **Applicant and**
(72) **Inventor: CHENG KIT YEW** [SG/SG]; Block 5#14-101 Normanton Park, Singapore 119002 (SG).

(81) **Designated States** *(unless otherwise indicated, for every kind of national protection available)*: AE, AG, AL, AM, AO, AT, AU, AZ, BA, BB, BG, BH, BR, BW, BY, BZ, CA, CH, CN, CO, CR, CU, CZ, DE, DK, DM, DO, DZ, EC, EE, EG, ES, FI, GB, GD, GE, GH, GM, GT, HN, HR, HU, ID, IL, IN, IS, JP, KE, KG, KM, KN, KP, KR, KZ, LA, LC, LK, LR, LS, LT, LU, LY, MA, MD, ME, MG, MK, MN, MW, MX, MY, MZ, NA, NG, NI, NO, NZ, OM, PG, PH, PL, PT, RO, RS, RU, SC, SD, SE, SG, SK, SL, SM, SV, SY, TJ, TM, TN, TR, TT, TZ, UA, UG, US, UZ, VC, VN, ZA, ZM, ZW.

(84) **Designated States** *(unless otherwise indicated, for every kind of regional protection available)*: ARIPO (BW, GH, GM, KE, LS, MW, MZ, NA, SD, SL, SZ, TZ, UG, ZM, ZW), Eurasian (AM, AZ, BY, KG, KZ, MD, RU, TJ, TM), European (AT, BE, BG, CH, CY, CZ, DE, DK, EE, ES, FI, FR, GB, GR, HR, HU, IE, IS, IT, LT, LU, LV, MC, MT, NL, NO, PL, PT, RO, SE, SI, SK, TR), OAPI (BF, BJ, CF, CG, CI, CM, GA, GN, GQ, GW, ML, MR, NE, SN, TD, TG).

Declaration under Rule 4.17:
— *of inventorship (Rule 4.17(iv))*

Published:
— *with international search report*

(54) **Title:** A CLEANING METHOD AND APPARATUS FOR REMOVING OIL, GREASE, CARBON, RUST AND COMBUSTION AMMUNITION RESIDUE FROM BARRELS OF ARTILLERY GUN, BATTLE TANK AND FIREARM.

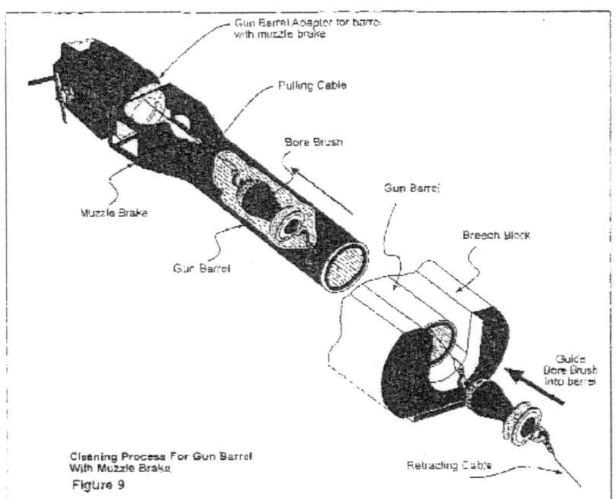

Cleaning Process For Gun Barrel With Muzzle Brake
Figure 9

(57) **Abstract:** The invention relates to a method and apparatus for cleaning gun barrels with or without muzzle brake of firearm, artillery and battle tank, whereby cleaning fluid, bore brush and a winch is used to remove carbon, grease, oil, rust and combustion ammunition residue from the barrel.

WO 2009/085013 A1

Patent Certificate for Vappro Automatic Barrel Cleaner

THE REGISTRY OF PATENTS
SINGAPORE

THE PATENTS ACT
(CHAPTER 221)

CERTIFICATE OF GRANT OF PATENT

In accordance with section 35 of the Patents Act, it is hereby certified that a patent having the P-No. 153707 has been granted in respect of an invention having the following particulars:

Title	:	A CLEANING METHOD AND APPARATUS FOR REMOVING OIL, GREASE, CARBON,RUST AND COMBUSTION AMMUNITION RESIDUE FROM BARRELS OF ARTILLERY GUN, BATTLE TANK AND FIREARM.
Application Number	:	200719154-7
Date of Filing	:	31 December 2007
Priority Data	:	-
Name of Inventor(s)	:	CHENG KIT YEW
Name(s) and Address(es) of Proprietor(s) of Patent	:	CHENG KIT YEW 39 PASIR PANJANG HILL # 03-01 GRANDHILL SINGAPORE 118860
Date of Grant	:	14 January 2011

Dated this 14th day of January 2011.

Danielle Yeow Pin Lin (Ms)
Deputy Registrar of Patents
Singapore

The author created the Vappro Automatic Barrel Cleaning Winch to turn the tedious problem of gun barrel cleaning into a business opportunity.

CHAPTER 36

Turning Problems into Opportunities Author's Case History 07

The problems in the gun barrel, which have been inherent prior to preservation without proper documentation of the condition of the barrel surface, has led to many unpleasant disputes between the armed forces and their contractors; this led to the invention of Vappro GBSS.

The only way to resolve a conflict is to address the root causes of the conflict and disagreement.

—Nelson Cheng

As mentioned in the preface of this book, the author's life-proven experience and innovative solutions to turning problems into opportunities are herewith illustrated over the next few chapters of his case studies.

Readers will learn about the background, genesis, problems, solutions, and detailed information of the author's invention, rationale, and process, as well as how some of the problems he encountered were turned into ground-breaking inventions that turned into profitable business opportunities.

The Invention of Vappro GBSS (Gun Barrel Surface Scanner)

The Background Leading to the Invention

The bore of the gun barrel needs to be checked or inspected quarterly for 'fit for firing', and this in accordance with the Preventive Maintenance and Corrective Serviceability Instructions and has been adopted by most armed forces worldwide.

Gun barrel surfaces have always been tedious to inspect. It's a process and an uphill task for soldiers. Visual inspection is not sufficiently effective currently. As the centre of the barrel is inaccessible, it lacks adequate light to assist the visual inspection. A simple and economical apparatus for visual inspection is needed.

The Genesis of the Invention

During the inspection, documentation of the condition of the gun barrel surface is necessary to enable an accurate examination of the said weapons, with the use of both eyes as a human would, with full depth perception.

Determine the Problems and Provide Solutions

This apparatus will provide detailed information on fouling, nicks, and pitting scourge, rifling-lifted, corrosion, major blemishes, heat-cracking, and erosion or excessive wear of the surface of the howitzer gun barrel and its exact location in the laptop computer.

An apparatus or device be of such a configuration is of utmost importance that a person can utilise the said apparatus or device to determine the exact location of the obstruction and/or the defect of the said barrel and have it documented in the computer during the inspection.

There are certain problems in the gun barrel, which have been inherent prior to preservation and, hence, preservation of said guns without proper documentation of the condition of the barrel; the surface has led to many unpleasant disputes between the armed forces and their contractors.

The author had personally experienced said disputes, and it had motivated the inventor to develop a system to resolve the above-said dispute, which resulted in the said invention.

A Detailed Description of the Invention

The invention of Vappro GBSS relates to an internal gun barrel surface scanner, used for scanning and inspecting the surface and the rifling of howitzer and main battle tank and gun barrel with a diameter ranging from 76 mm to 240 mm, and allowing the condition of the surface of the said barrels to be captured on the laptop computer, notebook computer, or portable personal computer for documenting purposes via a wireless view cam or miniature camera.

This scanner will provide detailed information on fouling, nicks, and pitting scourge, rifling-lifted, corrosion, major blemishes, heat-cracking, and erosion or excessive wear of the surface of the howitzer gun barrel and its exact location in the laptop computer.

According to the invention shown in figure 1, the internal bore gun barrel scanner consists of wireless IP camera, extendable inspection pole, tripod-like pole centering device, portable maintenance free dry battery, and portable personal computer.

Figure 2 shows how the extendable inspection pole is assembled via the male and female threaded pipe.

Figure 3 shows the process of how the tripod-like pole centering device is slogged onto the inspection pole.

Figure 4 shows the mounting of the wireless IP camera on the front end of the inspection pole powered by built-in dry cells.

Figure 5 shows the complete assembly of the internal bore barrel scanner.

Figure 6 shows the 360° scanning process of the internal bore barrel scanner with the aid of the pole-centering device.

Figure 7 shows how the inspection of the back portion of the bore of gun barrel is carry out via the breech block.

Figure 8 shows how the inspection of the front portion of the bore of gun barrel is carry out.

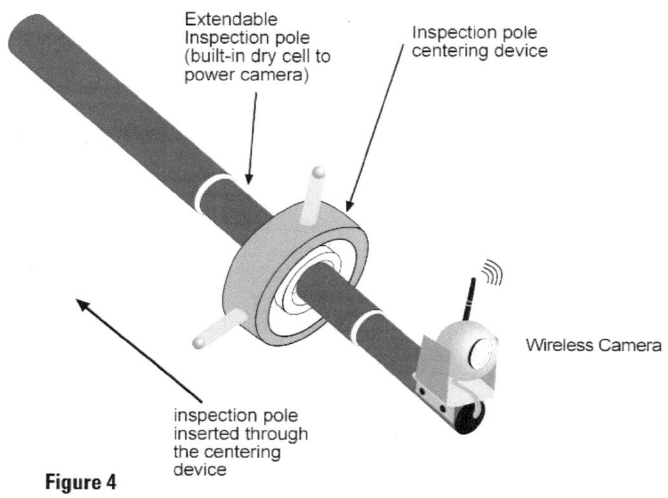

Figure 4

Figure 9 shows how up to twelve bores of the gun barrel can be inspected simultaneously via the scanner system software.

Figure 10 shows how the internal gun bore scanner wireless IP camera allows remote access from any web browser for real time image viewing through the Internet

The problems in the gun barrel, which have been inherent prior to preservation without proper documentation of the condition of the barrel surface, has led to many unpleasant disputes between the armed forces and their contractors.

The author had personally experienced said disputes, and it had motivated the author to develop an inexpensive system and yet effective to resolve above said dispute which resulted in the said invention.

Aiming to eliminate disputes between the armed forces and their contractors led the author not only to invent the Vappro GBSS, but also to obtain a patent for his invention.

We cannot achieve lasting peace in a just and equitable world unless we address the root causes of conflict and disagreement.

—Nelson Cheng

Patent Certificate for Vappro GBSS

THE REGISTRY OF PATENTS
SINGAPORE

THE PATENTS ACT
(CHAPTER 221)

CERTIFICATE OF GRANT OF PATENT

In accordance with section 35 of the Patents Act, it is hereby certified that a patent having the P-No. 157245 has been granted in respect of an invention having the following particulars:

Title	:	AN INTERNAL GUN BORE SURFACE SCANNER FOR INSPECTING AND RECORDING THE BORE CONDITION OF THE HOWITZER, MAIN BATTLE TANKS AND GUN BARREL WITH DIAMETER FROM 76 MM TO 240MM.
Application Number	:	200803946-3
Date of Filing	:	23 May 2008
Priority Data	:	-
Name of Inventor(s)	:	CHENG KIT YEW
Name(s) and Address(es) of Proprietor(s) of Patent	:	CHENG KIT YEW 39 PASIR PANJANG HILL #03-01 SINGAPORE 118860
Date of Grant	:	14 January 2011

Dated this 14th day of January 2011.

Danielle Yeow Pin Lin (Ms)
Deputy Registrar of Patents
Singapore

How can I apply the author's experience to my own company to turn a problem into an opportunity?

CHAPTER 37

Turning Problems into Opportunities Author's Case History 08

Due to the problems of environmental pollution caused by the production and use of anticorrosion packaging papers, Vappro VCI Mineral Stone Anticorrosion Paper was developed.

The effects of environmental pollution are incurable, the only solution to the problem is prevention.

—Nelson Cheng

The world needs to understand that humans can't live without Mother Earth, though the Mother Earth can do so without us.

—Nelson Cheng

Water and air, the two essential fluids on which all life depends, have become global garbage cans.

—Jacques-Yves Cousteau

The Invention of Vappro VCI Mineral Stone Anticorrosion Paper

The Background Leading to the Invention

The production and use of anticorrosion and packaging paper have several adverse effects on the environment that are collectively known as paper pollution. Pulp mills contribute to air pollution, water pollution, and land pollution.

As the third-largest industrial polluter of air, water, and land in both Canada and the United States, pulp and paper release well over 100 million kilograms of toxic pollution each year. Paper waste is also a major component of many landfill sites, accounting for approximately 35 per cent by weight of municipal solid waste (before recycling). In fact, even paper recycling contributes to pollution via the sludge left behind during deinking.

Paper and pulp are the fifth largest consumer of energy worldwide, consuming four percent of all energy used worldwide. To produce a ton of pulp and paper, the pulp and paper industry uses more water than any other industry.

Therefore, great care must be taken to ensure that the environment is protected during the production, use, and recycling or disposal of this enormous volume of material.

The author's research has long focused on finding an alternative to pulp-based anticorrosion paper, as it does not contain trees, water, chlorine, acids, or petroleum in its production. It is mainly composed of minerals such as calcium carbonate, one of the most abundant substances on earth, found within shells and pearls of marine organisms, or in the form of natural by-products of water and limestone quarries.

The Genesis of the Invention

To solve the above-described problems associated with the production of pulp-based paper the author researched the use of calcium carbonate, the commonest and most abundant mineral available on planet earth.

The composition of anticorrosion mineral paper comprising pulverised mineral powders including calcium carbonate, calcium silicate, calcium sulphate, barium sulfate, silica powder, chalk powder, dolomite powder, talcum powder, pulverised coal powder, kaolin, mica powder, zinc oxide, pigment, silicon dioxide, bentonite, clay, diatomite, and mixtures thereof, being subjected to calcination or not, anti-static agent, UV-resistant agent of mixture synergistic anticorrosion inhibitors that comprises of anodic, cathodic, adsorption, volatile corrosion inhibitors, and synthetic polymers binder that comprises of polyvinyl alcohol powders.

Determine the Problems and Provide Solutions

According to research, people cut down 15 billion trees each year, and the global tree count has fallen by 46 per cent since the beginning of human civilisation. Unless we realise the problems of cutting down trees, global warming will continue to rise.

Our lives depend on trees because they not only provide oxygen but also absorb carbon dioxide. Besides protecting us from flooding, they also maintain our land's beauty.

To minimise the cutting down of trees, necessary measures need to be taken. To prevent people from cutting down trees, we need to raise awareness among them about the benefits of trees.

Around the world, there should be frequent campaigns to raise awareness of the benefits of trees. By running these campaigns, we can explain why trees are important to us and why we should not cut them down. The message should be delivered using catchy and memorable words so that people can easily remember it.

Mankind cannot exist without trees, but the trees can exist without mankind.

—Nelson Cheng

Therefore, we should stop cutting trees and look for more environmentally friendly solutions to make paper to save our planet. This led to the invention of the Vappro VCI mineral stone paper.

The Detailed Description of the Invention

According to the aspect of the author's invention, it is the object of the invention to provide the chemical composition of the anticorrosion mineral paper comprising of a mixture of mineral powders, a mixture of synergistic corrosion inhibitors, anti-static agent, inorganic UV Inhibitors, and polymer-polyvinyl alcohol (PAV) powder or resin.

In an embodiment of the said invention, the mineral powders consist of calcium carbonate, calcium sulfate, calcium silicate, kaolin, barium sulfate, silica, bentonite, mica powder, zinc oxide, chalk powder, silica powder, talcum powder, and dolomite powder as a fillet for the mineral anticorrosion paper.

In another embodiment of the aid invention, a mixture of synergistic corrosion inhibitors is used to enhance the corrosion inhibition properties of the mineral paper. The combination of synergistic corrosion inhibitors such as anodic, cathodic, adsorption, volatile corrosion inhibitors, azole compounds, and phosphates are used to enhance the corrosion inhibition of the mineral paper.

Anodic corrosion inhibitors such as sodium silicate, sodium metasilicate, potassium silicate, sodium hepta silicate, hexaflurosilicates, molybdates, and orthophosphates are used as synergistic corrosion inhibitors to enhance the corrosion inhibition properties of the mineral paper.

The preferred anodic corrosion inhibitor is sodium silicate; it is a proven corrosion inhibitor, effective on a variety of metals, including tin, zinc, and copper. The preferred anodic corrosion inhibitor is sodium silicate because it reacts with metal surfaces to form a protective barrier against corrosion. It also increases water pH, another important corrosion control mechanism.

Cathodic corrosion inhibitors such as zinc salts, calcium salts, and magnesium salts are used to reduce the corrosion rate due to retarding cathodic reactions. The preferred cathodic corrosion inhibitor is calcium salts due to excellent compatibility in said chemical composition.

Adsorption inhibitors reduce the corrosion rate due to polarisation of the metal via an extremely thin layer of molecules being adsorbed on the surface. Decrease of the affective surface area results in reduction of the corrosion rate.

Adsorption inhibitors are substances (mainly organic) capable to form chemisorbed bonds with surface metal atoms. The following compounds are used as adsorption inhibitors amines (R-NH_2), carboxyls (R-COOH), thiourea (NH_2CSNH_2), phosphonates (R-PO_3H_2), and sodium benzoate ($C_7H_5NaO_2$).

The preferred adsorption corrosion inhibitor is sodium benzoate because of its excellent corrosion inhibition properties for steel, zinc, soldered joints, aluminium, and its alloys.

A solution to the pollution problems caused by the production of paper led to the invention and patent global application of the author.

There are many global threats that don't respect national boundaries, including environmental pollution, terrorism, and many others.

—Nelson Cheng

Pollution is comparable to terrorism.

—Nelson Cheng

Singapore Patent Granted

THE REGISTRY OF PATENTS
SINGAPORE

THE PATENTS ACT
(CHAPTER 221)

CERTIFICATE OF GRANT OF PATENT

In accordance with section 35 of the Patents Act, it is hereby certified that a patent having the P-No. 154349 has been granted in respect of an invention having the following particulars:

Title	:	COMPOSITION AND PROCESS OF MANUFACTURING OF BIODIESEL GREASE BY GELLING BIODIESEL, ANTI WEAR ADDITIVES, EXTREME PRESSURE ADDITIVES, WATER REPELLENT ADDITIVES AND ANTI-OXIDANT ADDITIVES.
Application Number	:	200800305 5
Date of Filing	:	11 January 2008
Priority Data	:	-
Name of Inventor(s)	:	CHENG KIT YEW
Name(s) and Address(es) of Proprietor(s) of Patent	:	CHENG KIT YEW 39 PASIR PANJANG HILL #03-01 SINGAPORE 118860
Date of Grant	:	15 June 2010

Dated this 15th day of June 2010.

Chiam Lu Lin (Ms)
Deputy Registrar of Patents
Singapore

A US Patent was filed

US 20180202110A1

(19) **United States**
(12) **Patent Application Publication**
CHENG KIT YEW

(10) **Pub. No.: US 2018/0202110 A1**
(43) **Pub. Date: Jul. 19, 2018**

(54) **CHEMICAL COMPOSITION FOR ANTI-CORROSION MINERAL PAPER**

(71) Applicant: **Nelson CHENG KIT YEW**, Singapore (SG)

(72) Inventor: **Nelson CHENG KIT YEW**, Singapore (SG)

(21) Appl. No.: **15/744,153**

(22) PCT Filed: **Jul. 31, 2015**

(86) PCT No.: **PCT/SG2015/050244**

§ 371 (c)(1),
(2) Date: **Jan. 12, 2018**

Publication Classification

(51) **Int. Cl.**

D21H 21/38	(2006.01)
D21H 17/00	(2006.01)
D21H 17/68	(2006.01)
D21H 17/67	(2006.01)
D21H 17/66	(2006.01)
D21H 17/36	(2006.01)
D21H 17/35	(2006.01)
D21H 17/09	(2006.01)

(52) **U.S. Cl.**
CPC ***D21H 21/38*** (2013.01); ***D21H 17/74*** (2013.01); ***D21H 17/68*** (2013.01); ***D21H 17/09*** (2013.01); ***D21H 17/66*** (2013.01); ***D21H 17/36*** (2013.01); ***D21H 17/35*** (2013.01); ***D21H 17/675*** (2013.01)

(57) **ABSTRACT**

The present invention relates to the chemical composition of an anti-corrosion mineral paper which consists mineral powders, anti-static agents, UV inhibitors, synergistic corrosion inhibitors and synthenic polymers binder.

Is there anything I can do to stop pollution?

CHAPTER 38

Turning Problems into Opportunities
Author's Case History 09

Many armed forces globally are struggling with manpower shortages due to downsizing and a declining population. This has forced them to explore more efficient methods of preserving and protecting their military equipment.

Population collapse is potentially the greatest risk to the future of civilization.

—Elon Musk

As urbanisation continues to expand at a rapid rate, aging and shrinking of the population have far-reaching implications for sustainability. The opportunity of implementing the solution without needing a large group of maintenance personnel to the armed forces appeared promising by recognising the challenges and opportunities presented by aging and shrinking urban populations.

The Development of VCI (Vapour Corrosion Inhibitor) Preservation Methodology for Armoured Vehicles, Battle Tanks, and Transport Vehicles over Cycles of Two Years

Background Leading the Invention

Original equipment manufacturers recommend that the armed forces change the oil in their land vehicles manually every three months to maintain operational readiness.

Due to shrinking manpower and declining populations, the armed services are having a tough time in the maintenance capabilities of their fleets of combat and transport vehicles.

Getting the engine started and running is also important. Repetition is necessary. Repeating the procedure every three or four weeks is time-consuming and tedious. The procedure involves various steps and accidents may occur.

To the army's dismay, it does not effectively keep the enemy at bay by maintaining battle tanks and armoured vehicles using this traditional method, because, over time, parts wear out and joints break down.

Corrosion occurs and rubber and electrical components deteriorate and require replacement. Replacement is required. Manhandling becomes too costly.

Humidity, moisture, and large temperature variations stemming from condensation take their toll on vehicles left to stand both indoors and outdoors. Gearboxes, engines, and even replacement parts are highly susceptible to changes in humidity. Weapon systems and electronic systems are prone to breakdowns if left in an atmosphere of uncontrolled humidity. Oil and grease cause degeneration over time when exposed to high humidity. This leads to the breakdown of components and severely reduces the life span of the vehicle.

Aging is a collective term for changes in the property of materials that occur on longer-term storage without the action of chemicals and controlling the humidity of the environment. This leads to partial or complete degradation, which occurs in the form of degradation processes and cracks formation.

Rubber seals are especially prone to such aging effects if left unprotected. The unsaturated groups in rubber present sensitivity towards oxygen, ozone, UV irradiation, bacteria attack, and other active substances. These reactions cause changes in the rubber seals and result in leakages of the hydraulic, fuel, and lubrication system

The Genesis of the Invention

In the author's invention, he invented a new method and incorporated the apparatus into the preservation of the above vehicles and equipment without experiencing the drawbacks previously referred to.

As a result of the problems mentioned above, he developed a method that protects the said vehicles from corrosion using vapour corrosion inhibitor products while at the same time reducing the need for manpower after the said vehicles and equipment are stored.

This invention reduced the amount of time or manpower required to change the engine oil of every vehicle every three to six months, which enhanced operational readiness and better-deployed soldiers in combat.

By providing complete preservation to the chassis, fuel system, lubrication system, cooling system, hydraulic system, electrical and electronic system, rubber parts, weaponry system, steering system, gearboxes, engines, optics, and exhaust system, said vehicles can be made operational.

Determine the Problems and Provide Solutions

The current method is an old-fashioned and tedious way that requires heavy dependence on physical manpower for maintaining the operational readiness of the the armed forces vehicles and equipment.

The author saw the need for developing a preservation method that could effectively protect military equipment and vehicles without suffering the drawbacks described above.

In response to the need, the VCI (vapour corrosion inhibitor) preservation methodology for armoured vehicles, battle tanks, and transport vehicles over a two-year cycle was developed.

The Detailed Description of the Invention

Described herein is the novel process as well as the VCI products used. The invention pertains to a VCI preservation scheme over a cycle of two years for main battle tanks, armoured vehicles, and transport vehicles employing a wide range of VCIs (vapour corrosion inhibitors).

In an embodiment of the invention as shown in figure 1, the preservation method consists of four methodological and detailed stages; the first stage beginning with zero-point maintenance is a compulsory service task that is conducted at the second stage before storage. The vehicle then undergoes the preparation stage of general cleaning, lubrication, and treatment of inherent corrosion.

The third stage involves the application of VCI products in the engine, differential and transfer case, steering system, engine transmission, final drives, cooling system, fuel the system, hydraulic system, exhaust system, optics, rubber components, electrical and electronic systems and connectors, weaponry system, suspension system, auxiliaries equipment, driver, crew compartment, and moving parts such as joints.

Once the VCI application is complete, the fourth stage involves sealing the entire vehicle, and then it will be covered with VCI canvas and kept in storage for two years before it is mobilised for operational purposes.

Another embodiment of the said invention is the zero-point maintenance, involving the change of engine lubricant, oil filters, fuel, fuel filters, gear lubricant, hydraulics oil, and if required, repairs to the vehicle to ensure its operational efficiency.

Another embodiment of the said invention is the preparation stage; it involves the cleaning of the interior and exterior of the vehicle with a VCI cleaning agent and the treatment of the inherent rust of the vehicle with VCI rust converter.

A further embodiment of the said invention involves the application of VCI products on all the essential systems and compartments of the vehicles spelled out below in the detailed preservation procedure of the vehicles.

By way of example and not limitation, the following are illustrative of various embodiments of the foregoing VCI preservation methodology for armoured vehicles, main battle tanks, and transport vehicle.

The details of the VCI preservation methodology of the armoured vehicles are herein described:

First Stage: Zero Point

Zero point involves the changing of engine oil, oil filters, steering oil, engine transmission oil, hydraulic fluids, fuel, and fuel filter.

Second Stage: Preparation of Vehicle

Clean the interior and exterior of armoured vehicle with water-based VCI degreaser.

Treat all existing corroded parts with VCI rust converter.

Lubricate door hinges and all moving parts of the vehicle with VCI grease.

Third Stage: Application of VCI Products on the Essential Systems of the Armoured Vehicle Engine

Drain out lubricating oil, refill with 90 per cent of new oil, and add 10 per cent of VCI oil additive via filler cap.

- **Transmission and Transfer Case.** Drain out lubricating oil, refill with 90 per cent of new oil, and add 10 per cent of VCI oil additives via transmission and transfer case filler plug.
- **Final Drives.** Drain out lubricating oil, refill with 90 per cent of new oil, and add 10 per cent of VCI oil additives via final drives filler plugs.
- **Swivel Housing Left and Right.** Drain out lubricating oil, refill with 90 per cent of new oil, and add 10 per cent of VCI oil additives via swivel housing filler plug.
- **Fuel System.** Top up VCI fuel additives (1 per cent of full tank capacity) into the fuel tank. Run the engine for three to five minutes at idling speed. A few times during the period, speed up the engine to top speed. Leave fuel lines filled with fuel fortified with VCI fuel additives. Do not remove fuel.
- **Rubber Components.** Apply silicon fluid on all rubber hoses and rubber parts.
- **Cooling System.** Drain out coolant, refill with 95 per cent of new coolant, and 5 per cent of VCI coolant additives.
- **Propeller Shafts.** Grease propeller shaft universal joints and sliding joints with VCI grease via all grease nipples.
- **Power Steering.** Drain out hydraulic fluid and refill with new fluid and add 5 per cent of VCI hydraulic additives.

- **Brake System.** Grease brake shoe adjuster, pivot points, and all brake linkages with VCI grease.
- **Clutch System.** Depress clutch paddle and insert the wooden block into the clutch lever. Spray VCI powder into the clutch chamber.
- **Vehicle Road Test.** Start engine, drive for 1 km, and check for leaks.
- **Electrical System.** Relay box. Spray all connectors in the relay box with VCI electro spray and install VCI emitter. Spray starter motor solenoid contact point with VCI electro spray.
- **Power Distribution Box.** Spray all connector's contact points with VCI electro Spray and install VCI foam emitter.
- **Connectors.** Spray all connectors with VCI electro spray and install VCI emitter.
- **Slave Receptacle.** Coat slave receptacle with VCI wax.
- **Battery Terminal.** Remove cable connection point from battery and coat with VCI wax. Return battery to authority for maintenance.
- **Starter Motor.** Lubricate starter motor pinion gear with VCI grease.
- **Exhaust System.** Spray exhaust pipe with VCI oil additives. Coat external exhaust pipe with VCI rust converter. Seal exhaust opening with VCI film, security label, and aluminium foil tape.
- **Crew Cabin.** Apply silicon fluid to all rubber and plastic parts. Install VCI foam emitternear to instrument.
- **Tracks.** Apply VCI silicone fluid to all rubber pads and apply VCI wax on all track links.

Fourth Stage: Sealing of Vehicle

Seal the openings (between cabin and crew compartment) with VCI film and aluminium foil tape. Place security seal at all openings. If the vehicle is to be preserved outdoor or without shelter, cover it with a VCI canopy.

Routine Inspection during Storage at One-Year Point

External chassis. Inspect the conditions of the enclosure. Carry out sealing on the enclosure if required. Inspect hinges and re-oil if necessary.

Internal chassis. If inspection is required for crew compartment, break security seals and enter vehicle. Open all doors and ventilate for at least five minutes before entering so that fresh air can circulate through the cabin. Inspect the interior of the vehicle for signs of deterioration, and carry out necessary maintenance works if required. Special attention must be given to checking the floorboard for water condensation. Drain condensate if necessary. Inspect every rubber seal and treat them with VCI silicon fluid if necessary. Replace VCI at every second annual inspection—alternatively, after twenty-four months if the vehicle has not been opened for interior inspection.

After body, the interior has been inspected and re-preservation completed, ensure that all the openings are properly (re)sealed with security label seal.

Re-Preservation of Armoured Vehicle after Mobilisation

General. All equipment should be cleaned and dried, followed by inspection before reapplying of VCI products. Water trapped in the vehicle should be removed.

Static mobilisation. If it is just only static mobilisation, i.e., only to start the engine for less than half an hour, then re-application of new VCI products is not necessary. You may recycle the existing used VCI products. However, it is of paramount importance to seal all opened openings with new sealing tapes and security label seals.

Moving/open mobilisation. If the vehicle is mobilised for a few days, please repeat the procedures above.

A problem of aging and shrinking populations faced by the military was turned into a profitable opportunity through VCI's preservation of methodology, once again turning a problem into an opportunity. The said development led to the patent being granted in Singapore and Taiwan.

Singapore Patent Granted

THE REGISTRY OF PATENTS
SINGAPORE

THE PATENTS ACT
(CHAPTER 221)

CERTIFICATE OF GRANT OF PATENT

In accordance with section 35 of the Patents Act, it is hereby certified that a patent having the P-No. 159428 has been granted in respect of an invention having the following particulars:

Title	:	VCI (VAPOR CORROSION INHIBITOR) PRESERVATION METHODOLOGY OF ARMORED VEHICLES, BATTLE TANKS, AND TRANSPORT VEHICLES OVER CYCLES OF TWO YEARS.
Application Number	:	200806870-2
Date of Filing	:	02 September 2008
Priority Data	:	-
Name of Inventor(s)	:	CHENG KIT YEW
Name(s) and Address(es) of Proprietor(s) of Patent	:	CHENG KIT YEW 39 PASIR PANJANG HILL #03-01 SINGAPORE 118860
Date of Grant	:	15 December 2011

Dated this 15th day of December 2011.

Tan Yih San
Registrar of Patents
Singapore

Taiwan Patent Certificate

Certificate of Patent of Republic of China

Invention Patent No. I432695

Title of Invention Patent: VCI (Vapor Corrosion Inhibitor) Preservation Methodology of Armored Vehicles, Battle Tanks, and Transport Vehicles Over Cycles of Two Years

Patentee: CHENG, KIT YEW 新加坡 SG

Inventor(s): CHENG, KIT YEW

Duration Term of Patent: **From:** **April 1, 2014**
To: **September 10, 2028**

Pursuant to the Patent Law, the patentee is entitled to grant the patent right.

Intellectual Property Office
Ministry of Economic Affairs
Director General

Issuance Date: **April 1, 2014**

(Note 1: The patent right will lapse, if patentee does not pay the maintenance fee before the dead line. – **March 31** annually thereafter)

Considering the shrinking and aging population, what can I do?

CHAPTER 39

Turning Problems into Opportunities Author's Case History 10

Paper and pulp mill owners throughout the world are looking for a more efficient way to clean continuous digesters as the existing mechanical method is too time-consuming and costs owners millions of dollars during the annual shutdown.

How much you save is as important as much you make because a cent saved is equal to a cent gained.

—Nelson Cheng

A cent saved equals a cent gained, so a cent saved is the same as a cent made.

—Nelson Cheng

Saving a cent equal making a cent, thus saving a cent is the same as earning a cent.

—Nelson Cheng

Almost all pulp and paper digesters are cleaned with mechanical grinders and brushes that are abrasive and cause wear to the surfaces, which results in a metal loss. The author designed a system to eliminate such problems without the use of mechanical grinders or brushes.

Background Leading to the Invention

Maintenance shutdowns cost the industry millions of dollars each year in maintenance costs, and mill owners are required to cover these costs because of downtime.

In today's globalised economy, higher maintenance costs lead to higher costs. Mill owners are forced to raise prices due to inflation to clean digesters more efficiently. The author's invention addresses this issue.

Compared to mechanical cleaning, this invention offers significant advantages in terms of reducing downtime, manpower requirements, costs, and damage.

The Genesis of the Invention

Wood chips contain organic and inorganic materials such as sodium, calcium, silica, potassium, aluminium, etc. The combined effect of these components together with cooking chemical liquor sludge will result in scaling, which affects the cooking process of the pulp due to reduced flowrate.

The current method of cleaning the digester of the pulp and paper mills is a tedious and dangerous process that requires many man-hours. Often, workers must work at heights of up to 50 m.

The digesters are cleaned by means of very high-pressure jet washers and mechanical grinders. This laborious and time-consuming method makes use of mechanical grinders and hard brushes which is abrasive. Naturally, it also causes wear of the surfaces of the digester, thus causing extensive metal loss.

The said method is a tedious and dangerous process that involves at least fifteen to twenty men to be stationed inside the digester, exposing the workers to the risk of an industrial accident due to the elevated work area and poorly lighted interior of the digester.

The hard scales of the internal surface of the digester are cleaned by means of mechanical contact of the brush and surface grinder in rotation movement. Men deployed to carry out such tasks often experience injury due to overstrained muscles.

Also, the current method requires men to be stationed inside the digester for a considerable length of time up to ten to twelve days on shift rotation, making it an extremely tedious and difficult task.

The intention of the present invention is to create a new kind of method of cleaning for the digester without experiencing the drawbacks referred to above.

A special object of the invention is to develop an effective cleaning method by removing the scale of the digester through boiling out the digester with inhibited acid scale and rust remover and high-pressure water jet washing.

It involves the use of Magna 113, an inhibited acid scale and rust remover fortified with corrosion inhibitor and a high-pressure jet washer ranging from 200 bars up to 2,500 bars, drastically reducing the downtime for cleaning digester from an average of eleven days to 3 days.

A further object of the invention is to enhance the daily production yield of the digester by thoroughly cleaning the screens using the said invention.

Detailed Description of the Invention

In accordance with this invention, it is an object of the invention to provide the details of the digester-cleaning process using the chemical boiling out of the digester inhibited acid scale and metal cleaner, and its equipment.

The example of cleaning a continuous cooking digester with a volume of 500,000 L of mill water and its cleaning process is herein described.

Preparation of Chemicals and Equipment

1. Type of chemical for descaling: Magna 113 an inhibited acid scale and metal cleaner; quantity required: 50,000 L.
2. Type of chemical for flushing the screen and neutralisation of the inhibited acid scale remover and metal cleaner are 10 per cent of sodium hydroxide solution (commonly known as white liquor in pulp and paper industries), 30,000 L for each screen.
3. Using double boiling out circulation pump with a flow rate of 900 m^3 per hour to fill the digester with approximately 500 m^3 of mill water as shown in figure 1 marked in blue.
4. Installation of chemical tank of twenty-five tons capacity and chemical transfer pump with a flow rate of 150 m^3 per hour. Fill up the chemical tank with inhibited acid scale and metal cleaner from the baby tank. Transfer the chemical from the chemical tank into the digester via digester manhole by using said chemical transfer pump as shown in figure 2 marked in blue. With said installation, the boiling out of the upper and lower screen of the digester can be carried at the same time with approximately thirty-six hours of circulation time as shown in figure 3 marked in blue.

Cleaning Procedure

1. Empty black liquor from the digester.
2. Take some sample of black liquor from the blow-down line of the digester for analysis for iron contents, total dissolved solids, and pH.
3. Flushing and draining of each screen of the digester with mill water.
4. Take a water sample from each digester screen for analysis for iron contents, total dissolved solids, and pH.
5. Fill the digester with approximately 500 m^3 mill water by using boiling out circulation pump.
6. Transfer inhibited acid scale remover and metal cleaner from a baby tank of into the twenty-five tons chemical tank and then transfer the chemical into the digester via digester manhole by using chemical transfer pump as shown in figure 2. The estimated time required for the said process is approximately two hours.
7. Start descaling digester screens for thirty-six hours by using double boiling out circulation pump as shown in figure 3 marked in blue.

The total time required for cleaning the digester and the process involved is detailed as follows:

By using the author's invention, downtime for digester cleaning has been drastically reduced, from an average of eleven days has been shortened to three days.

The technology saves mill owners millions of dollars by transforming the tedious, time-consuming, and potentially dangerous process of digester cleaning into a profitable business opportunity.

His invention was subsequently granted a patent.

A Singapore Patent Granted

THE REGISTRY OF PATENTS
SINGAPORE

THE PATENTS ACT
(CHAPTER 221)

CERTIFICATE OF GRANT OF PATENT

In accordance with section 35 of the Patents Act, it is hereby certified that a patent having the P-No. 158774 has been granted in respect of an invention having the following particulars:

Title	:	A CLEANING METHOD AND PROCEDURES FOR CLEANING CONTINOUS DIGESTER OF PULP & PAPER
Application Number	:	200805577-4
Date of Filing	:	23 July 2008
Priority Data	:	-
Name of Inventor(s)	:	CHENG KIT YEW
Name(s) and Address(es) of Proprietor(s) of Patent	:	CHENG KIT YEW 39 PASIR PANJANG HILL #03-01 SINGAPORE 118860
Date of Grant	:	31 December 2010

Dated this 31st day of December 2010.

Liew Woon Yin (Ms)
Registrar of Patents
Singapore

Is there a specific methodology I should use to reduce costs in my company?

CHAPTER 40

Turning Problems into Opportunities Author's Case History 11

The invention of Lupromax EA heat-activated technology (HAT) additives.

Every setback of a product provides an opportunity for improvement.

—Nelson Cheng

Setbacks for a particular technology provide the opportunity for new innovations.

—Nelson Cheng

The petroleum crude and poly alfa olefins (PAO) and their lubrication properties are directly linked to the stability of their viscosity. The lubricant loses its lubricating properties when its viscosity thins down due to heat. There is therefore a need to find a solution to the heat issue in lubrication.

The Invention of Lupromax EA Heat-Activated Technology (HAT) Oil Additives

The Background Leading to the Invention

Most of the conventional and synthetic lubricants used in automotive and industrial machinery are refined from petroleum crude and poly alfa olefins (PAO), and its lubrication properties are directly linked to the stability of its viscosity.

Heat causes the viscosity of said lubricants to thin down, which impacts their performance as lubricants, which are detrimental to machinery performance. It is therefore of paramount importance to maintain a stable viscosity for petroleum-based and synthetic lubricants.

The Genesis of the Invention

As metal surfaces of machinery move relative to one another, friction between the two surfaces converts kinetic energy into heat energy. It can have dramatic consequences on the moving parts, causing scarring, galling, and seizures. Friction causes kinetic energy to be converted to heat.

During his quest to eliminate friction from modern machinery and utilise friction-generated heat, the author developed heat-activated lubrication technology (HAT).

Detailed Description of the Invention

It provides heat-activated lubrication technology (HAT) that utilises heat generated from friction to activate a sulphurized and chlorinated compound in oils, solvents, and grease-like lubricant carriers to polarise the metal surfaces, forming microfilm protection on the metal surfaces, which prevents it from seizing, scarring, and galling when loaded, thereby enhancing its load-carrying capacity.

When said mediums are subjected to excessive friction due to an increase in temperature, the chemical compound increases its load-carrying capacity significantly.

However, the increasing demand for higher machine performance has also led to more heat being generated, inevitably thinning down the viscosities of the conventional lubricants, resulting in more operational failure of machinery.

The term *lubricant* generally refers to lubricating materials that are applied as fluids. To be effective, a lubricant must maintain sufficient film thickness to carry the load while keeping friction and wear at a minimum. The lubricant must also cool moving parts by absorbing and carrying away the heat produced by friction.

A lubricant's thickness is generally determined by its viscosity, temperature, and load. Viscosity is a measure of an oil's thickness. Greater film thickness is usually associated with higher viscosity lubricants. Using lubricants with too high viscosities will, however, increase frictional load and energy consumption.

If the lubricant viscosity is too low, film thickness will be reduced, and machinery wear will increase. Lubricant viscosity is affected by operating temperature. As the temperature rises, the lubricant tends to become thinner and loses its lubricant properties, resulting in excessive wear to the metals and ultimately seizure of moving parts.

The lubricant must be formulated with additives to meet the demands of modern machinery, but conventional lubricant additives only increase the viscosity index of oil, but as load and temperature increase, the lubricant becomes ineffective.

In heat-activated lubrication technology, heat-activated chemicals react with metal surfaces to form a micro protective film. The author's inventions contains a blend of vegetable fatty acids, extreme pressure agents, corrosion inhibitors, anti-wear agents, and antioxidants. Chemicals that activate under heat are used to achieve the results.

Friction directly converts energy into heat. This heat is caused by asperities that protrude from moving parts caused by microscopic collisions that penetrate the oil film. The asperities break off when the ordinary oil is used, forming wear metals that can be seen in used oil.

When activated by heat, the EP agent in this invention fuses/attaches itself to ferrous metal surfaces by changing their molecular structure. Pores are thus sealed, smoothing out any asperities without affecting tolerances.

Since the film is exceptionally strong and its thermal modification ability enables most of the asperities to bend or fold by internal yield-type flow in the direction of impact, it is not susceptible to breaking. In addition, they usually flatten out into their normal plane of shear, which is usually cylindrical or flat.

The flattening greatly increases the total area of potential contact between the two surfaces, which makes it easier for the load to be distributed. A combination of at least one of these might lead to a greater load-carrying capacity or longer wear. Timken Load machine motor-monitoring ammeters indicate that this effect tends to lower friction coefficient.

The heat-activated lubrication technology combines vegetable fatty acids, a pressure agent, a corrosion inhibitor, and antioxidants with petroleum-based products. Heat-activated chemicals are used to achieve the desired lubrication results.

Several studies demonstrate that heat-activated chemicals such as sulphurized and chlorinated compounds will polarise on the surfaces of heated metals, forming a micro protective film that will protect it against galling, scarring, and seizure of moving parts.

The composition of the heat-activated technology is herein described.

The technology of heat-activated lubrication combines extreme pressure agents, anti-wear agents, lubricity agents, antioxidants, corrosion inhibitors, and mineral oils.

Heat-activated chemical oil additives include sulfonated or amine-based corrosion inhibitors and aminic antioxidants, which are added in small amounts to mineral oil as a lubricant.

Naphthenic or paraffinic mineral oils of C-14 to C-18 carbon chains can be used.

The additives combined with the anti-wear additives can either be phosphorus or chlorine based. To enhance its lubricity properties, an ester lubricity agent is used.

Antioxidant properties are provided by corrosion inhibitors and aminic antioxidants.

After being treated with Lupromax EA oil additives, the above synergistically blended chemicals produced excellent amazing heat-activated technology (HAT) that was recorded in an Indonesia Guinness World Record for running a car without lubricant of up to 280 km without lubrication.

In subsequent years, a patent was granted, and the heat-activated technology (HAT) trademark was granted globally. The said invention has won the prestigious Korea Consumers Satisfaction Award.

Certificate of Patent for Singapore

THE REGISTRY OF PATENTS
SINGAPORE

THE PATENTS ACT
(CHAPTER 221)

CERTIFICATE OF GRANT OF PATENT

In accordance with section 35 of the Patents Act, it is hereby certified that a patent having the P-No. 156546 has been granted in respect of an invention having the following particulars:

Title	:	COMPOSITION AND METHOD OF MANUFACTURE OF HEAT ACTIVATED CHEMICAL BIODIESEL BASED OIL ADDITIVE.
Application Number	:	200803165-0
Date of Filing	:	24 April 2008
Priority Data	:	-
Name of Inventor(s)	:	CHENG KIT YEW
Name(s) and Address(es) of Proprietor(s) of Patent	:	CHENG KIT YEW 39 PASIR PANJANG HILL #03-01 SINGAPORE 118860
Date of Grant	:	31 October 2011

Dated this 31st day of October 2011.

Tan Yih San
Registrar of Patents
Singapore

Indonesia Guinness World Record for running a car without lubricant of up to 280 kilometers without lubrication

REKOR DUNIA

PIAGAM PENGHARGAAN
MUSEUM REKOR-DUNIA
INDONESIA
No. 5407/R.MURI/IV/2012
Dianugrahkan Kepada
PT. Magna Indonesia
(LUPROMAX)
ATAS REKOR
Ketahanan Mobil dan Motor
Berjalan tanpa Pelumas terlama
Mobil : 283.8 Km - 8 Jam 5 Menit
Motor : 242.8 Km - 8 Jam 10 Menit
Semarang, 29 April 2012

JAYA SUPRANA

HAT Registered Trademarks

WIPO | MADRID
The International Trademark System

CERTIFICATE OF REGISTRATION

The International Bureau of the World Intellectual Property Organization (WIPO) certifies that the indications appearing in the present certificate conform to the recording made in the International Register of Marks maintained under the Madrid Agreement and Protocol.

Reproduction of the mark	HAT HEAT ACTIVATED TECHNOLOGY
Registration number	**1 206 505**
Registration date	**April 17, 2014**
Date next payment due	**April 17, 2024**
Name and address of holder	MAGNA INTERNATIONAL PTE LTD 10H Enterprise Road, Singapore 629834 (Singapore)
Legal nature of the holder (legal entity) and place of organization	Private Limited Company
Classification of figurative elements	27.5
Description of the mark	The word mark device is an invented work mark device and cannot be found in the English dictionary; "HAT" is coined after the words Heat Activated Technology.
List of goods and services NCL(10-2013)	4 Lubricants and oil additives for automotives and industrial applications.
Basic registration	Singapore, 08.04.2013, T1306000A
Designations under the Madrid Protocol	China, European Union, India, Japan, Mexico, Republic of Korea, United States of America
Declaration of intention to use the mark	India, United States of America
Date of notification	19.06.2014
Language of the international application	English

Ásta Valdimarsdóttir
Director, Operations Service
Madrid Registry
Brands and Designs Sector

Geneva, June 19, 2014

WORLD INTELLECTUAL PROPERTY ORGANIZATION

34, chemin des Colombettes
1211 Geneva 20, Switzerland
www.wipo.int

Korea Consumers Satisfaction Award

제2017-07034호

대한민국소비자만족도 1위

KOREA CONSUMER SATISFACTION AWARDS

수상 부문 : 차량용품(엔진오일첨가제)
기 업 명 : 루프로맥스코리아 주식회사
브랜드 명 : LUPROMAX-EA

귀사는 품질, 서비스, 사후관리 등 실질적 소비자 만족도 평가에서 두각을 나타내고 건전한 소비문화 정착에 기여하였으므로 대한민국 소비자 만족도1위로 선정되었습니다.

2017년 7월 11일

KCSA 운영사무국

주최 Korea Marketing Forum Inc. 한국 마케팅 포럼 후원 ChosunMedia 조선일보

<<Korea Consumers Satisfaction Award>>

Trophy for Korea Consumers Satisfaction Award

How can I overcome my current setbacks?

CHAPTER 41

Turning Problems into Opportunities
Author's Case History 12
A special tribute to my dad, Comdt Cheng Kim Bing, and mum, Woo Wei Kheng.

Problems, adversities, and hardships often prepare ordinary people for extraordinary success.
—Comdt Cheng Kim Bing
(translation of Dad's wise saying from Cantonese)

We must have hope that tomorrow will be better than today in order to move forward in life.
—Madam Woo Wei Kheng
(translation of Mom's wise saying from Cantonese)

As a special tribute to my late beloved parents, who were exemplary giant problem-solvers, this book ends with a chapter dedicated to them. I will never forget their resilience in raising nine children and taking care of my grandma from extreme poverty and hardship.

Despite living in such cramped quarters with twelve members of my family, my parents and siblings were happy. Subsistence living has taught us to be content with what we have.

Even though they struggled every month to pay electrical bills, rent, school fees, groceries, etc., somehow they managed to provide us with all our basic needs because of their sheer hard work and resilience.

The legacy of love and resilience instilled in us by our parents has helped us to become street-smart successful adults today.

Following are some valuable quotes that have become my pillar of reference when dealing with life's problems and while resolving them.

Neither mental strength nor resiliency can be obtained by winning,
but by facing hardships and overcoming challenges.
—Comdt Cheng Kim Bing
(translation of Dad's wise saying from Cantonese)

In general, ordinary people who overcome hardships and difficulties can achieve extraordinary success.

—Comdt Cheng Kim Bing
(translation from Dad's wise saying from Cantonese)

It is through trials and hardships that mental strength and resiliency are built.

—Comdt Cheng Kim Bing
(translation of Dad's wise saying from Cantonese)

A great father, a trusted friend, a spiritual counsellor, and a business advisor, my dad was all those things and more. His wisdom was superior to that of most of his contemporaries because he was well-read and knowledgeable. A kind, forgiving, patient, and magnanimous person, he was kind to everyone around him.

Introduction

The village of Yong Mark, in Guangdong, China, was the place where my father was born in 1920. As my dad was eight years old, my grandfather moved to Singapore in search of greener pastures, leaving behind two sons and his wife.

The Trip to Singapore

When Dad was thirteen, he decided to leave his village for Singapore in search of a job. It took a week of seasickness to complete the journey.

My dad first arrived in Singapore when it was a sleepy fishing village. It was filthy and narrow. Infestations of cockroaches, houseflies, and bed bugs plagued the houses. Malnourished immigrants and their children dominated the population. There were many cases of tuberculosis and other diseases. The consumption of opium was widespread.

Arrival in Singapore

When he arrived in Singapore, he joined my grandfather's printing firm as an apprentice. Rather than learning the art of linotype letterpress printing, he was assigned general tasks. In those days, apprentices were considered the lowest in a company's hierarchy and often mistreated by senior workers.

Despite my grandfather's position as shop foreman, my dad had no special privileges. Instead, he was neglected and was not taught the necessary skills.

An Industrious and Resilient Father

While the other workers went home in the evening, he would spend another hour studying linotype and letterpress printing by observation and practice. Eventually, he became one of the best linotype letterpress printers because of his diligence and desire to learn.

In the daytime, he worked hard at the printing company, then rushed home to do chores before going to night classes. On 15 February 1942, the Japanese invaded Singapore, ending this routine.

A Resourceful Father

He learned the Japanese language during the Japanese occupation, gaining an alternative source of income. He soon became a British translator.

Eventually, he had enough money to buy a house and a factory in Bukit Timah. However, when the Americans bombed Hiroshima and Nagasaki, the Japanese surrendered, rendering the banana money worthless overnight. Dad had to work as a linotype operator until he retired.

A Responsible Dad

He married in his early twenties, became a father of nine children (five boys and four girls), and became a responsible father. To support the family, he worked two jobs. He would leave for work at 7.00 a.m., be home by 5.00 p.m., and leave for his night job shortly after. His routine remained the same for more than twenty-five years.

A Caring and Nurturing Dad

He was a caring and nurturing father. Despite being busy with his work, he made time for the children, taking us for rides on his scooter every evening. While riding around the Queenstown neighbourhood, he would always have two children with him.

An Amazing Father Who Would Lay Down His Life for His Family

He was a father who was willing to give his life for his family. I remembered an incident that occurred during the racial riots in the sixties when the chaos spread to the area of Forfar House. My father wore his Red Cross boots and armed himself with an axe as he bravely guarded the perimeter of the house while ushering us into the house. Thankfully, the police arrived on time, and the rioters dispersed without incident.

Dad, All in All

Dad was a great father, friend, spiritual advisor, and a business adviser. Knowledgeable and well-read, he was wiser than many of his contemporaries. He treated those around him with kindness, patience, forgiveness, and magnanimity.

His Children and Grandchildren Were Blessed by This Loving Father and Grandfather

At my wedding, he prayed for my wife and I, blessing us as we served tea to our parents and elder relatives during the traditional Chinese tea ceremony. He named my daughter Sook Han, which means 'filial', and my son Weng Tuck, which means 'righteous'. When my children visited him, he regularly laid hands on them and prayed for them, and he never once reprimanded them for misbehaving.

Mentor and Father Who Is Farsighted and Inspiring

Dinner with my parents was a regular occurrence for me and my wife. The dinner table was an occasion for us to discuss anything and everything under the sun on these occasions. We would hear from him about his past experiences and his views on global and economic issues.

Years before China became the world's second-largest economy, he spoke about global depression cycles, the economy, and even predicted the rise of China. In addition to inspiring me to enter the world of business, he taught me the importance of being practical with financial resources. He taught me to embrace sound business principles and life lessons.

Rapid Promotion to the Rank of Commander

Dad joined the Singapore Red Cross Society to help the community and quickly learned first aid during the weekends. By applying his newly acquired skills to many of our neighbours, he soon became a very popular first aider among our neighbours.

He was promoted to the rank of commander because of his passion for first aid. The Singapore Red Cross Society commander often had the opportunity to meet with foreign dignitaries throughout the world, including Queen Elizabeth II, Prince Philip, Princess Anne, etc.

Offered a Position as Aide-de-Camp

Ultimately, Dad was offered a post of aide-de-camp president of Singapore, but he personally felt that his English was insufficient for the post, so he politely declined the offer.

Godly Father

After retirement dad prayed daily for his family, his church, and the government. His mornings were spent reading and praying. Magna, its staff, and all pending projects will be prayed for. The afternoon will be spent studying the Bible for Sunday classes. He gave his best to the church and was an excellent Sunday school teacher.

A Passionate Father

It was my dad's passion to learn and acquire new skills. The sixty-eight-year-old graduated from Bible school and learned to play the guitar at sixty-six.

He retired at seventy after suffering a second heart attack, but remained active in the church, teaching Sunday school as long as he was physically able.

Deteriorating Health

Dad had his first heart attack at the age of forty-nine; the hardships he had experienced in his early years began to affect his health. Despite his illness, he lived a full and productive life until he was eighty-two years old.

His heart stopped three times during his third heart attack, but he was resuscitated each time. I was in the intensive care unit with my brother Dickson. 'Take care of your siblings and your mother,' he said in a weak voice. After that, he blessed us with a prayer.

In the meantime, two other brothers were returning from overseas after learning about my dad's condition. His faith in God gave him the strength to endure until the entire family returned to Singapore.

The following day, he miraculously recovered and was able to return to his normal ward. This was an incredible testimony to the hospital's doctors and nurses.

Many comments were made by the nurses, including 'A miracle', 'God's healing', and 'Your dad was a good patient.

The Cheng Kim Bing-UABC Postgraduate Scholarship was created in his honour and in his memory.

My Tribute to Mom, Madam Woo Wei Kheng

My beloved mum the matriarch of the family was called home to be with the Lord on 22 June 2017.

Surrounded by her children and grandchildren praying and singing her favourite hymns, her passing was serene and peaceful, indicating the presence of the Lord was with her.

Mum lived a full life of ninety-one years of age and was blessed with four generations of offspring. She will always be remembered for her love, patience, godliness, and care for others. She was a caring and loving mother, grandmother, and great-grandmother, who was well-loved by her family, neighbours, and friends.

My mother grew up in an underprivileged family. Her adopted family treated her badly, but she was always gracious and harboured no grudges against them or other people who mistreated her.

Years later, she raised her own family closely knitted and left behind her legacy of love.

A Godly Mother

Mum expressed her love for God in a unique way. Every morning, she would hold a glass of water facing the sky to give thanks to God, appreciating God for his blessings upon her family. She would then pray for the entire clan of fifty-six members.

Mum showed deep concern for us through her prayers whenever we travelled overseas; she would keep praying till we had returned home safely.

An Intelligent and Creative Woman

Despite her good academic inclinations, Mum's adopted mother stopped her education while she was still in primary school. She served as a model student and was a class monitor during her few years.

Mum excelled in the kitchen, recreating and reinventing recipes with a personal touch. She always ensured that we ate well. She was also creative and artistic in her handiwork and enjoyed singing and music.

A Generous and Magnanimous Woman

Mum was always generous in her giving to the needy and to her four generations of offspring. She would give *angbaos* (money packaged in a small red envelope) to her children, grandchildren, and great-grandchildren during their birthdays and Chinese New Year.

Legacy of Love

Mum left behind the true meaning of love, magnanimity, and generosity to her four generations of off springs.

She is a mother that I hope my wife and daughter would emulate.

Though we miss her physical presence, we will hold on to her fond memories and her legacy till we meet her again at the heavenly gates.

About the Author

The author is the founder and chairman of the Magna Group, which encompasses Magna International, Magna Chemical Canada Inc., Magna Australia Pvt Ltd, and Lupromax International Pte Ltd. In addition, he is a senior honorary research fellow at the Autonomous University of Baja, California.

A leading inventor in Singapore, he has filed more than twenty-five patents and more than fifteen trademarks both locally and abroad.

A total of more than 500 products have been invented by him including heat-activated technology (HAT) lubricants, vapor biocorrosion inhibitors (VBCI), molecular reaction surface technology (MRST), colloidal corrosion inhibitors (CCI), silver nanoparticles hospital grade disinfectants to combat hospital-acquired infections (HAIs), and more.

Over 230 of his inventions have received NATO Stock Numbers and have been marketed in more than thirty countries.

He has won numerous international awards for his packaging inventions, including the World Packaging Association's (WPA) President God Award, several World Packaging Excellence Awards, numerous Asia Packaging Federation (APF) Awards for packaging excellence, and many Singapore Star Awards for sustainable packaging.

Among his achievements is the Lupromax EA engine oil additive. This additive has been incorporated into the Indonesia World Record Museum after running cars and motorcycles without lubrication for 280 km and eight hours. He is a pioneer of the Legionella-X disinfectant, which kills 100 per cent of the H5N1 avian flu virus.

As an author and editor, he has co-authored three books: *Vappro VBCI: The Solution to Corrosion Control*, *Legionella-X Disinfectants: Fighting Infectious Diseases*, and *Vappro VBCI: Mothballing Reference Book*.

Having published 140 research papers and technical journals—in journals such as the National Association of Corrosion Engineers (NACE), International Journal of Emerging Technology and Advanced Engineering (IJETAE), International Journal of Current Trends in Engineering & Technology (IJCTET), Cambridge University Press, Academia.edu, ResearchGate, and Intech Open—and co-authored books on anticorrosion and combating infectious diseases, as well as the mothballing of onshore and offshore equipment.

Among his many awards, he was the first Singaporean to win the 2020 World Packaging Star and the President Gold Award for green and sustainability products.

Winner of the 2020 Asia Packaging and Singapore Star Packaging Awards for Green Packaging; 2015 Winner of the Asia Packaging Award; Top 10 Most Inspiring Entrepreneur 2015; Winner of the Global Star, Asia Star, and Singapore Star Packaging Awards 2014, 2015, 2016, 2017, 2014; Top Entrepreneur Award-Singapore Small Medium Business Association; Asia Excellence Award 2014; and Top 20 Innovation Award 2013 from Small Medium Business Association.

Member of the National Association of Research Fellows (NARF) Australia, Society of Tribologists and Lubrication Engineers (STLE), American Chemical Society (ACS), World Corrosion Organization (WCO), and European Federation of Corrosion (EFC). Served on the committee of the Singapore Packaging Council.

A man was born with the capability of creating and manifesting things not possible before he arrived.

—Nelson Cheng

CPSIA information can be obtained
at www.ICGtesting.com
Printed in the USA
LVRC081320160422
716078LV00031B/330

* 9 7 8 1 5 4 3 7 6 8 9 2 3 *